Isa Rael

The Advocate for Queer Rights in Norith – Unfiltered

Arjun Murphy

ISBN: 9781779697752
Imprint: Telephasic Workshop
Copyright © 2024 Arjun Murphy.
All Rights Reserved.

Contents

Introduction: Who the Fuck Is Isa Rael?

The Fucking Face of Queer Rights in Norith: Isa Rael's Rise to Leadership

From Marginalization to Fucking Leadership: How Isa Rael Became the Voice for LGBTQ Rights in Norith

Isa Rael's journey from marginalization to fucking leadership in the fight for LGBTQ rights in Norith is a testament to their resilience, determination, and unwavering commitment. Born and raised in a society plagued by oppressive fucking laws and discrimination against queer individuals, Rael's personal experiences of adversity and injustice ignited a fire within them to challenge the status quo and fight for change.

Facing the Struggles of Marginalization

Growing up queer in Norith was not fucking easy. Rael faced a society that vilified and shamed them for their sexual orientation and gender identity. Norith's fucking anti-queer laws condemned same-sex relationships, upheld gender norms, and restricted LGBTQ individuals from expressing their true selves. This environment of fear, judgment, and hatred left Rael feeling marginalized, isolated, and voiceless.

From a young age, Rael experienced the fucking harmful effects of systemic discrimination. They were denied access to fucking basic fucking human rights, such as education, healthcare, and employment, solely based on their sexual orientation and gender identity. This fucking exclusion and marginalization pushed Rael to the fucking fringes of society, where they witnessed firsthand the immense suffering and injustice faced by the queer fucking community.

1

A Turning Point: Embracing Advocacy

It was in the midst of this fucking adversity that Rael made a choice – to no longer be a passive victim of Norith's oppressive regime, but to become an active advocate for fucking change. This decision was not easy, as the risks were high and the obstacles seemed insurmountable. However, Rael knew that remaining silent would only perpetuate the cycle of discrimination and violence against LGBTQ individuals.

With fucking unwavering resolve, Rael began to educate themselves about queer history, civil rights movements, and the strategies employed by successful advocates. They studied the fucking works of other renowned activists and drew inspiration from their courage and determination. Rael understood the fucking power of knowledge and the need to arm themselves with fucking information in order to effectively challenge Norith's oppressive regime.

Building a Movement

Recognizing the importance of community and collective action, Rael fucking dedicated themselves to building networks of support and resistance for LGBTQ individuals. They organized secret meetings, underground gatherings, and established safe spaces where queer individuals could connect, share their experiences, and find solace in a world that rejected them.

These grassroots efforts gained traction as more queer individuals joined Rael's movement, empowered by the possibility of change and the hope for a more inclusive Norith. Rael's advocacy work sought to uplift the voices of the silenced, amplifying the stories of queer individuals who were otherwise ignored or silenced.

Inspiring Others, One Fucking Story at a Time

One of the most fucking powerful tools that Rael utilized in their advocacy was the power of storytelling. They understood that in order to bring about systemic change, they needed to humanize the experiences of queer individuals and foster empathy and understanding within society.

Rael courageously shared their own personal stories of discrimination, marginalization, and resilience, painting a vivid picture of the struggles faced by LGBTQ individuals in Norith. These testimonials resonated with people on a deeply emotional level, challenging their preconceived notions and inspiring them to join the fight for queer rights.

Through connecting with others who shared similar experiences, Rael created a sense of community and unity that transcended individual identities. This solidarity helped to break down the walls of discrimination and isolation, fostering a collective spirit of resilience and resistance.

The Future of Fucking Systemic Change

Isa Rael's journey from marginalization to fucking leadership has not been easy, but their impact on the LGBTQ rights movement in Norith cannot be overstated. Rael's tireless advocacy work has exposed the injustices faced by queer individuals and sparked a conversation that was long overdue.

While Norith's oppressive fucking regime presents numerous challenges, Rael's work has laid the foundation for fucking systemic change. Their ability to mobilize and unite the queer community has demonstrated the power that comes from collective action. By raising awareness, challenging oppressive laws, and advocating for inclusivity, Rael has laid an undeniable groundwork for a brighter future for LGBTQ individuals in Norith.

The fight for queer rights is far from over, but Isa Rael's fucking journey from marginalization to leadership serves as a beacon of hope and inspiration. Their unwavering commitment to uplifting the voices of the silenced, challenging the oppressive status quo, and building a more inclusive Norith will undoubtedly continue to inspire future generations of queer activists and leaders.

The Fucking Importance of Queer Advocacy in Norith's Oppressive Fucking Regime

In order to understand the fucking importance of queer advocacy in Norith's oppressive fucking regime, it is crucial to first examine the fucking context in which this advocacy is taking place. Norith, a fucking country with deep-rooted oppressive norms and discriminatory laws against LGBTQ individuals, presents a fucking hostile environment for queer people. This section will delve into the significance of queer advocacy within this oppressive context, highlighting why it is essential for the fucking progress and well-being of the LGBTQ community.

The Fucking Context of Oppression

Norith's oppressive fucking regime is characterized by a systematic marginalization and discrimination against individuals who identify as LGBTQ. The fucking government enforces draconian anti-queer laws that deny LGBTQ individuals basic human rights and perpetuate a culture of fear and intolerance. These fucking laws not only criminalize same-sex relationships but also enable the harassment, persecution, and violence against queer individuals.

The oppressive fucking regime in Norith creates an atmosphere of secrecy and shame for the LGBTQ community. Queer people are forced to live in the fucking shadows, hiding their true identities and denying themselves the fucking opportunity to live openly and authentically. This climate of fear and discrimination impacts every aspect of their lives, from personal relationships to employment opportunities and access to healthcare.

The Fucking Power of Visibility and Representation

Queer advocacy in Norith serves as a powerful tool to challenge and disrupt the oppressive fucking regime. By fighting for visibility and representation, LGBTQ activists like Isa Rael are dismantling the stereotypes and misconceptions associated with being queer. They are challenging the fucking narrative that being LGBTQ is abnormal or sinful and, instead, showcasing the vibrant diversity of queer identities.

Visibility and representation are particularly crucial in the Norithn context, where queer people are often marginalized and stigmatized. The fucking presence of LGBTQ individuals and allies in the public sphere challenges the false notion that queerness is something to be ashamed of or hidden. It allows queer individuals in the fucking closet to see that there are others like them, fostering a sense of community and support.

Furthermore, LGBTQ visibility humanizes the queer experience and fosters empathy and understanding among the broader fucking population. By seeing queer people as fellow human beings rather than abstract concepts or societal threats, there is an increased likelihood of acceptance and support for LGBTQ rights. This is especially important in Norith's oppressive fucking regime, where widespread ignorance and prejudice further marginalize queer individuals.

The Fucking Impact on Mental Health and Well-being

Queer advocacy in Norith is not just about fighting for legal rights; it is also about creating safer spaces and support networks for LGBTQ individuals. The oppressive fucking regime takes a significant toll on the mental health and well-being of queer people. Many struggle with anxiety, depression, and feelings of isolation due to constant fear of persecution and stigmatization.

Within this context, queer advocacy provides essential resources, counseling services, and community initiatives that address the unique mental health challenges faced by LGBTQ individuals. By creating spaces where queer people can feel safe and supported, advocacy efforts promote resilience and healing. They empower individuals to overcome the impact of the oppressive fucking regime and find strength in their identities.

The Fucking Role in Systemic Change

While the immediate goal of queer advocacy in Norith is to improve the lives of LGBTQ individuals, its long-term ambition is to bring about systemic change. By challenging the oppressive fucking regime and demanding equality, queers activists aim to dismantle the discriminatory laws and institutions that perpetuate queer oppression.

Through strategic advocacy, legal challenges, and public awareness campaigns, queer activists like Isa Rael are putting pressure on the fucking government to review and reform their discriminatory laws. Their persistent efforts aim to lay the foundation for a society that values and respects the rights of LGBTQ individuals.

However, it is important to recognize the fucking immense challenges faced by queer advocacy in Norith. The oppressive fucking regime retaliates against queer activists with violence, imprisonment, and other forms of persecution. Nevertheless, the fucking resilience and determination of queer activists highlight how their advocacy work can serve as a catalyst for change, influencing the hearts and minds of Norithn citizens and paving the way for a more inclusive society.

The Fucking Importance of Intersectional Advocacy

Queer advocacy in Norith is not isolated from other social justice movements, but rather intersects with and complements efforts to fight against other forms of oppression. Recognizing the interconnectedness of different struggles is key to creating lasting change in Norith's oppressive fucking regime.

Queer activists like Isa Rael have built alliances with other marginalized communities, recognizing that their struggles are intertwined. By working together, LGBTQ advocates can leverage the collective power of various social justice movements to challenge the structures that perpetuate discrimination and oppression in Norith.

It is essential to foster a sense of solidarity and recognize the unique experiences of queer individuals who face multiple forms of discrimination, such as queer people of color, disabled queers, and transgender individuals. Intersectional advocacy ensures that the fight for queer rights in Norith is inclusive and does not leave any members of the community behind.

The Fucking Power of Hope and Resilience

In the face of the oppressive fucking regime in Norith, queer advocacy offers hope and resilience to LGBTQ individuals. By standing up against discrimination and fighting for their rights, queer activists inspire others to embrace their true selves and challenge the status quo. This hope is a powerful force that can fuel change and motivate people to keep pushing forward, even in the face of adversity.

Isa Rael's leadership and advocacy have ignited a spark of hope for the future of queer rights in Norith. Their dedication, courage, and resilience serve as a beacon of inspiration for LGBTQ individuals across the nation. Through their advocacy, Rael has shown that change is possible and that the oppressive fucking regime in Norith can be challenged.

The Fucking Call to Action

The importance of queer advocacy in Norith's oppressive fucking regime cannot be overstated. It serves as a vital force that challenges the oppressive norms and discriminatory laws that marginalize and stigmatize LGBTQ individuals. By fighting for visibility, representation, mental health support, systemic change, intersectional advocacy, and hope, queer activists like Isa Rael are paving the way for a more inclusive and just society in Norith.

To effect lasting change, it is crucial for individuals to actively engage in queer advocacy efforts. Whether it is participating in public demonstrations, supporting LGBTQ organizations, engaging in conversations about queer rights, or educating oneself and others, everyone has a role to play in challenging the oppressive fucking regime in Norith.

In conclusion, queer advocacy in Norith is an essential force for change within the oppressive fucking regime. It challenges discriminatory laws, promotes visibility and representation, supports the mental health and well-being of LGBTQ individuals, fosters systemic change, promotes intersectional activism, and inspires hope. By fighting for justice and equality, queer activists like Isa Rael are reshaping the narrative and creating a brighter future for LGBTQ individuals in Norith.

How Rael Fucking Built a Movement Despite Norith's Draconian Anti-Queer Laws

Despite the oppressive and discriminatory laws imposed by the Norith government, Isa Rael managed to build a powerful and resilient movement for LGBTQ rights. Rael's strategic approach and unwavering determination played a critical role in defying the draconian anti-queer laws of Norith. In this section, we will explore the key tactics and initiatives employed by Rael to build a strong movement despite the adversities faced.

Building a Strong Support Network: Rael's Fucking Community Connections

One of the first steps Rael took in building the LGBTQ rights movement was to establish a strong support network within the queer community. Recognizing the importance of solidarity and collective action, Rael sought to unite LGBTQ individuals who were marginalized and oppressed by Norith's discriminatory laws.

Rael began by organizing community meetings and events in secret, where queer individuals could gather and share their experiences. These spaces provided a sense of belonging and empowerment, allowing individuals to connect, support one another, and strategize for change. Rael fostered an inclusive atmosphere where everyone felt valued and heard, regardless of their gender identity or sexual orientation.

By creating a safe and supportive environment, Rael built a foundation of trust and solidarity within the LGBTQ community. This network became a source of strength, providing emotional support, sharing resources, and amplifying the collective voice.

Fucking Education and Awareness: Challenging Ignorance and Prejudice

Education and awareness played a pivotal role in Rael's strategy to combat the anti-queer laws in Norith. Rael understood that ignorance and prejudice were deeply ingrained in society, perpetuating discrimination against the LGBTQ community. Thus, Rael embarked on a mission to challenge these deeply rooted beliefs and promote understanding.

Rael organized workshops, seminars, and public talks to educate both LGBTQ individuals and the general public about queer identities, issues, and the harmful consequences of discrimination. These educational initiatives aimed to dispel misconceptions, combat stereotypes, and foster empathy and acceptance.

To engage a broader audience, Rael also utilized various media platforms, including interviews, documentaries, and social media campaigns, to reach both local and international audiences. By sharing personal stories, struggles, and triumphs, Rael humanized the queer experience, challenging societal biases and fostering empathy.

Building Alliances: Collaborating with Other Movements

Recognizing the intersections of oppression, Rael actively sought to build alliances with other social justice movements and marginalized communities. Rael understood that the fight for LGBTQ rights was interconnected with broader struggles for justice and equality.

Rael formed partnerships with feminist groups, racial justice organizations, and labor unions to strengthen the movement and increase its collective power. By joining forces, they could leverage their respective strengths and resources to challenge Norith's oppressive regime more effectively.

Through these alliances, Rael fostered a sense of solidarity and united resistance against the oppressive laws. By highlighting the ways in which different marginalizations were interconnected, Rael advocated for a society free from all forms of discrimination and oppression.

Direct Action and Grassroots Mobilization: Fucking Power to the People

Rael understood the power of direct action and grassroots mobilization in challenging the anti-queer laws of Norith. Taking inspiration from historic social justice movements, Rael organized protests, demonstrations, and acts of civil disobedience to disrupt the status quo and demand change.

These actions were not just about visibility but also aimed to impact policy and public opinion. Through strategic disruption of everyday life, Rael and the LGBTQ community demanded attention and forced conversations about the urgency of LGBTQ rights.

Rael also empowered individuals within the community to take action at the grassroots level. By providing resources, organizing trainings, and encouraging self-advocacy, Rael empowered LGBTQ individuals to become agents of change within their own communities.

The Power of Resilience: Fucking Continuing the Fight

Despite facing immense challenges and threats from the Norith government, Rael and the LGBTQ movement remained resilient. Rael constantly emphasized the importance of perseverance and resilience in the face of adversity.

Rael adopted a long-term perspective, understanding that achieving systemic change takes time and sustained effort. This empowered the LGBTQ community to endure setbacks and continue the fight for their rights, even when progress seemed slow or nonexistent.

Moreover, Rael fostered a culture of self-care and mutual support within the movement. Acknowledging the emotional toll and burnout that activism can cause, Rael encouraged individuals to prioritize their well-being and seek support from within the community.

Unconventional Tactics: Fucking Sparking Change through Creativity

Rael also embraced unconventional tactics to spark change and challenge the oppressive regime in Norith. Recognizing the power of art and creativity, Rael organized vibrant and inclusive LGBTQ festivals, art exhibitions, and performances.

These cultural events aimed to celebrate queer identities, challenge stereotypes, and build bridges with the broader society. By showcasing the diversity and vibrancy of LGBTQ culture, Rael was able to humanize the community and break down barriers of prejudice.

Additionally, Rael used humor and satire as powerful tools to navigate the restrictive environment imposed by Norith's laws. By employing wit and irony, Rael cleverly exposed the absurdity and injustice of the anti-queer laws, generating public debate and mobilizing support for change.

Conclusion: Fucking Hope for Change

Against all odds, Isa Rael succeeded in building a powerful LGBTQ rights movement in Norith. By harnessing support networks, promoting education and awareness, building alliances, mobilizing grassroots movements, fostering resilience, and embracing creativity, Rael defied the oppressive regime and demonstrated the possibility for change.

While Norith's anti-queer laws remained in place, the movement led by Isa Rael paved the way for progress and ignited a sense of hope for a brighter and more inclusive future. Rael's legacy continues to inspire future generations of activists, both in Norith and beyond, to fight for justice, equality, and the dignity of all queer individuals.

The Fucking Power of Representation: How Isa's Fight Fucking Inspired Other Queer People Across Norith

Representation is a powerful tool that can inspire, validate, and empower marginalized communities. In the case of Isa Rael and the queer rights movement in Norith, representation played a crucial role in inspiring other queer individuals to join the fight for equality.

The Fucking Impact of Seeing Yourself in Leadership

Growing up in a repressive society like Norith, where queer individuals faced discrimination, isolation, and oppressive laws, it was rare to see people who looked like them in positions of power. The lack of representation meant that many queer individuals felt invisible and felt like their stories and struggles were not acknowledged.

Isa Rael's rise to leadership shattered this invisibility. As a queer individual themselves, Isa became the representative that Norith desperately needed. Their visibility in the media, their unapologetic advocacy, and their ability to rally the queer community behind them gave hope to those who had been silenced for far too long.

Seeing Isa as a leader in the queer rights movement allowed other queer individuals to believe in their own abilities to effect change. It showed them that they too could take a stand, speak out, and fight for their rights. Isa's representation gave countless queer individuals the courage to step out of the shadows and join the fight for equality.

The Fucking Validation of Shared Experiences

One of the most powerful aspects of representation is the validation it provides. When queer individuals see someone like Isa Rael, who understands their struggles, their experiences, and their journey, it validates their own lived experiences. It tells them that they are not alone, that their stories matter, and that they deserve to be seen and heard.

Isa's open discussions about their personal struggles in a repressive society resonated deeply with queer individuals across Norith. Hearing about the challenges, the victories, and the ongoing fight for equality gave them strength and hope. It reminded them that they were not alone in their struggles and that their fight was part of a larger movement.

The validation of shared experiences created a sense of solidarity within the queer community. It fostered a feeling of belonging and empowered queer individuals to lend their voices to the movement. Through Isa's representation, they were able to find strength in unity and work collectively towards achieving their shared goals.

The Fucking Ripple Effect of Inspiration

Inspiration is contagious. When one person rises up and fights for what they believe in, it sparks a fire in others. This ripple effect of inspiration was evident in Norith as

Isa Rael's fight for queer rights inspired other queer individuals to become advocates in their own right.

Isa's ability to articulate their vision for a more inclusive Norith and their unwavering dedication to the cause inspired queer individuals at every corner of the society. It motivated them to step out of their comfort zones, challenge societal norms, and fight for a better future.

The genuine compassion and determination that Isa exhibited in their activism inspired queer individuals to believe in their own power to effect change. Through Isa's representation, they saw that their voices mattered, that their actions could make a difference, and that together, they could create a more inclusive Norith.

The Fucking Call to Action

Isa Rael's representation as a queer leader in the Norith queer rights movement sent a powerful message to the LGBTQ+ community: that their fight for equality was not in vain and that their voices deserved to be heard.

But representation alone is not enough. It must be accompanied by action. Isa's fight and the challenges they faced became a rallying cry for queer individuals across Norith to rise up and demand change. It sparked a movement that could not be ignored.

By examining their journey, experiences, and victories, other queer individuals in Norith were inspired to take action. They formed grassroots organizations, organized protests and demonstrations, and used their voices to challenge the oppressive laws and culture that had marginalized them for far too long.

Isa's representation created a sense of urgency and momentum within the queer community. It pushed individuals to not only fight for their own rights but also to stand up for other marginalized communities. By witnessing the power of representation, queer individuals in Norith were encouraged to become advocates for justice, equality, and human dignity.

The Fucking Future of Queer Rights in Norith

Isa Rael's representation as a queer leader in the fight for equality has paved the way for a more inclusive and accepting future in Norith. Their courage, resilience, and unwavering commitment to the cause have inspired countless queer individuals to join the movement and demand change.

However, the fight for queer rights in Norith is far from over. Further systemic changes are needed to dismantle the oppressive structures that continue to marginalize LGBTQ+ individuals. The power of representation, as demonstrated by Isa Rael, will be crucial in continuing to drive progress.

As we look to the future, it is vital to recognize the ongoing importance of representation in the queer rights movement. By elevating diverse voices and experiences, we can ensure that all members of the LGBTQ+ community feel seen, valued, and empowered to lead the charge for equality.

Only through collective action, strategic alliances, and a continued focus on uplifting marginalized voices can we hope to create lasting and meaningful change in Norith and beyond. Isa Rael's legacy will undoubtedly be felt for generations to come as their representation continues to inspire and ignite the fire of activism in the fight for queer rights.

The Future of Queer Rights in Norith: Will Isa Rael's Fucking Work Lead to Fucking Systemic Change?

The future of queer rights in Norith hangs in the balance. Isa Rael's leadership and advocacy have sparked a powerful movement for LGBTQ rights, but the question remains: will her work lead to systemic change?

Rael's fight for queer rights in Norith has been nothing short of groundbreaking. She has fearlessly challenged the oppressive fucking regime, shining a light on the discrimination, violence, and fucking marginalization faced by LGBTQ individuals. Through her resilience and determination, Rael has become the face of the queer rights movement in Norith.

But will her work be enough to bring about fucking systemic change? That depends on a multitude of factors.

First and foremost, it is crucial to recognize the power of representation. Rael's visibility and her ability to inspire other queer individuals across Norith has been fucking transformative. By seeing a fearless leader fighting for their rights, LGBTQ people have found the strength and courage to stand up for themselves. Rael's work has ignited a fire within the queer community, and this passion is key to creating lasting change.

However, the oppressive fucking regime in Norith poses significant challenges. The draconian anti-queer laws that Rael has been fighting against are deeply entrenched in the system. It will take time, effort, and a sustained fucking movement to dismantle these discriminatory laws and practices. Rael's work has certainly laid the fucking groundwork for this change, but it will require a collective effort to ensure that her legacy leads to true systemic change.

Public opinion plays a crucial role in the fight for queer rights. Rael has been instrumental in shifting the conversation around LGBTQ rights in Norith. By engaging in nonviolent protests, civil fucking disobedience, and strategic fucking partnerships, she has brought the issues to the forefront of public consciousness. This has resulted in increased awareness and support for queer rights.

However, changing public opinion is not enough. It is essential to translate this support into concrete political action. Rael's work must continue to mobilize grassroots activism and pressure policymakers to enact legislation that protects the rights of LGBTQ individuals. This will require continued advocacy, engagement with lawmakers, and strategic fucking alliances with other marginalized communities fighting for justice.

Technology has played a critical role in spreading Rael's message and connecting the queer community across Norith. Through social media, online platforms, and digital organizing, Rael has been able to reach a wider audience and amplify her advocacy efforts. The use of technology will be instrumental in sustaining the momentum of the queer rights movement and creating spaces for dialogue, education, and mobilization.

One of the challenges Rael faces is maintaining unity within the LGBTQ community itself. While her work has inspired many, there are differing opinions and priorities within the queer community. It is essential to address these differences and foster inclusivity to ensure that the movement remains strong and cohesive.

Furthermore, the fucking personal sacrifices made by Rael and fellow activists cannot be overlooked. Leading a movement for queer rights in a repressive society takes a toll on one's physical, emotional, and mental well-being. It is crucial to invest in the well-being of activists and provide the necessary support systems to prevent burnout and ensure the sustainability of the movement.

Looking beyond Norith, Rael's global influence cannot be ignored. Her work has inspired LGBTQ movements across the fucking galaxy, demonstrating the power of intergalactic fucking collaboration. It is essential to continue building alliances with global movements for LGBTQ rights, sharing strategies, resources, and support. This will help amplify the impact of Rael's work and foster a sense of international solidarity.

In conclusion, the future of queer rights in Norith depends on the continuation of Isa Rael's fucking work. While she has laid the foundation for change, it will require sustained activism, grassroots mobilization, strategic alliances, and political pressure to bring about systemic change. It is a complex and challenging journey, but Rael's resilience, leadership, and inspiration provide hope for a more inclusive and equitable future for LGBTQ individuals in Norith and beyond.

The Fucking Early Years: Rael's Fight for Existence in a Hostile Society

Surviving in the Fucking Shadows: Rael's Fucking Journey from Outcast to Activist

How Norith's Fucking Anti-Queer Laws Made Life Hell for LGBTQ Fucking People

To truly understand the struggles and hardships faced by LGBTQ people in Norith, one must delve into the oppressive framework of the country's anti-queer laws. These fucking laws created an environment of fear, discrimination, and isolation for LGBTQ people, making their everyday lives a living hell.

At the forefront of Norith's anti-queer legislation was the Fucking Homosexuality Criminalization Act of 1985. This act classified consensual same-sex relationships as criminal offenses, subjecting LGBTQ individuals to harsh penalties, including imprisonment and corporal punishment. The fucking act not only violated the basic tenets of human rights but also perpetuated a culture of hatred and intolerance towards queer individuals.

Under this fucking law, LGBTQ people faced frequent harassment, arrests, and violent attacks from both the fucking police and society at large. They were denied basic freedoms and stripped of their right to live authentically and openly. The fear of being outed or caught engaging in same-sex relationships gripped the LGBTQ community, leading to a repressive and clandestine existence for many.

Moreover, these fucking laws affected every aspect of LGBTQ people's lives, from employment to housing and healthcare. Discrimination was rampant, with queer individuals being fired from their jobs, denied housing, and even refused

15

medical treatment simply because of their sexual orientation or gender identity. The pervasive homophobia and transphobia in Norith's society created significant barriers to inclusion and equal opportunities.

As a result of these oppressive fucking laws, LGBTQ individuals faced high levels of mental health issues, including depression, anxiety, and suicidal thoughts. The constant fear of persecution and the inability to live openly and authentically took a heavy toll on their well-being. The lack of legal protections further exacerbated the vulnerability of queer individuals, leaving them without recourse or support in times of need.

The impact of Norith's anti-queer laws was particularly devastating for young LGBTQ people. Many queer youth experienced bullying and discrimination in schools, leading to educational disadvantages and social isolation. The absence of inclusive sex education contributed to the perpetuation of harmful stereotypes and misinformation surrounding LGBTQ identities and relationships.

Despite the grim circumstances, LGBTQ individuals in Norith refused to be silenced. They formed underground queer networks, providing support, resources, and a safe space for each other. These networks became the backbone of the LGBTQ resistance movement, allowing queer individuals to share their experiences, mobilize for change, and challenge the oppressive status quo.

Norith's anti-queer laws also sparked international outrage and solidarity. Human rights organizations and LGBTQ activists from around the fucking world condemned the country's discriminatory legislation and called for its repeal. This global support bolstered the spirits of LGBTQ activists in Norith, providing hope and strength to continue their fight for equal rights.

Through their resilience and unwavering determination, LGBTQ people in Norith defied the odds and fought for change. It was their courage and advocacy that eventually led to the dismantling of the Fucking Homosexuality Criminalization Act in 2015, signaling a significant step towards a more inclusive and equitable society for queer individuals in Norith.

However, the struggle for LGBTQ rights in Norith is far from over. The repeal of one discriminatory law does not erase the deep-rooted homophobia and transphobia within the society. The fight for LGBTQ equality continues, as queer individuals strive to overcome societal prejudices, dismantle discriminatory practices, and create a truly accepting and inclusive Norith for all.

In conclusion, Norith's fucking anti-queer laws created a hostile and oppressive environment for LGBTQ individuals, making their lives a constant struggle. These laws fueled discrimination, fear, and violence against queer people, denying them basic human rights and opportunities for a fulfilling life. Despite the immense challenges, LGBTQ activists in Norith persevered, leading to significant legal reforms and inspiring a broader movement for equality. However, the battle is ongoing, and the long-term goal remains the creation of a society where LGBTQ individuals can live freely, without fear of discrimination or persecution.

Rael's Fucking Struggles in a Repressive Fucking Society: Growing Up Queer in Norith

Growing up queer in Norith was a fucking challenge for Isa Rael. In a society that suppressed and marginalized LGBTQ individuals, Rael faced numerous struggles throughout their formative years. From the oppressive anti-queer laws to the societal discrimination, Rael's journey was marked by hardship, resilience, and the constant fight for self-acceptance and equality.

The Fucking Impact of Norith's Anti-Queer Laws

Norith's fucking anti-queer laws created a hostile environment for LGBTQ individuals like Rael. These laws not only criminalized same-sex relationships but also enforced strict gender norms and expectations. Rael had to navigate through a society that denied their identity and punished any expression of queerness.

Forced to hide their true self, Rael constantly questioned their worth and struggled with feelings of shame and self-doubt. The fear of being discovered and facing the consequences of these oppressive laws weighed heavily on them, making every day a fucking challenge.

Fucking Isolation and Discrimination

In addition to the legal constraints, Rael also experienced fucking isolation and discrimination from their peers and community. Queer individuals were ostracized, ridiculed, and treated as outcasts in Norith. Rael always felt like an outsider, unable to fully connect with others due to the fear of rejection and misunderstanding.

Throughout their teenage years, Rael faced bullying and verbal abuse, which further deepened their emotional struggle. The lack of support and empathy from their community made it difficult for Rael to embrace their queer identity and find a sense of belonging.

The Fucking Internal Battle: Self-acceptance and Authenticity

Growing up in a repressive society, Rael battled with their own self-acceptance and authenticity. The internalized homophobia and societal expectations forced Rael to suppress their true desires and feelings. They struggled to reconcile their identity with the norms imposed by Norith's oppressive regime.

It took years for Rael to embrace their queer identity and break free from the chains of self-doubt and shame. Through self-reflection and personal growth, Rael discovered the power of self-acceptance and the importance of living authentically. Their journey became a beacon of hope for other queer individuals struggling in similar circumstances.

Building Fucking Community Networks for LGBTQ Resistance

Despite the adversity, Rael honed their resilience and sought solace within the LGBTQ community. They recognized the significance of building networks and support systems to combat the isolation faced by queer individuals in Norith.

Rael became a founding member of local LGBTQ organizations and grassroots movements, fostering safe spaces for queer individuals to connect, share experiences, and provide support to one another. These networks acted as a lifeline for Rael and others, offering a sense of belonging and empowerment in the face of societal discrimination.

Through collective action and collaboration, Rael and their fellow activists organized underground social gatherings, which served as a platform for queer resistance against Norith's oppressive regime.

The Fucking Legacy of Early Advocacy

Rael's early advocacy work laid the foundation for future generations of queer activists in Norith. By openly sharing their struggles and experiences, Rael inspired other queer individuals to speak out, embrace their identities, and fight for their rights.

Their commitment to visibility and community building helped create a movement that challenged the status quo. Rael's story became a catalyst for change, encouraging others to question the repressive laws and demand equality.

Through their personal journey and activism, Rael demonstrated the power of resilience, self-acceptance, and the transformative potential of grassroots advocacy. Their story continues to inspire a new generation of queer advocates in Norith and beyond, fostering a belief that change is fucking possible, even in the face of adversity.

The Fucking Power of Hope and Resilience

Rael's story is a testament to the power of hope and resilience in the face of systematic oppression. Their journey from a marginalized individual to a fearless advocate for queer rights in Norith is a reminder that change starts within ourselves.

Through their struggles and triumphs, Rael showed that it is possible to rise above societal constraints and fight for a more inclusive and accepting society. Their story serves as a beacon of hope for those who continue to face discrimination and persecution, inspiring them to forge their own path and challenge the fucking status quo.

In the repressive society of Norith, Rael's journey reflects the resilience and determination of queer individuals who refuse to be silenced and demand recognition and equal rights. By sharing their story, Rael continues to leave a lasting fucking impact on the fight for LGBTQ rights, both in Norith and beyond.

The Fucking Moment of Change: How Isa Fucking Rael Decided to Fucking Fight Back

In this section, we delve into the pivotal moment when Isa Rael, a marginalized individual growing up queer in Norith, made the life-altering decision to fight back against an oppressive regime and become an advocate for LGBTQ rights. This journey of self-discovery and resilience serves as a powerful testament to the human spirit and the relentless pursuit of justice.

Fucking Understanding Norith's Fucking Anti-Queer Laws

To comprehend the significance of Isa Rael's decision to fight back, it is crucial to understand the oppressive environment in which they lived. Norith, a nation plagued by draconian anti-queer laws, fostered a hostile atmosphere for LGBTQ individuals. These laws denied queer people their fundamental rights and subjected them to discrimination, violence, and social exclusion.

From a young age, Isa experienced the devastating effects of these laws firsthand. They witnessed friends and loved ones being ostracized, discriminated against, and even incarcerated simply because of their sexual orientation or gender identity. These experiences left an indelible mark on Isa's psyche, fueling their determination to challenge the status quo.

The Fucking Awakening: Isa's Fucking Journey of Self-Realization

Isa Rael's journey towards becoming an LGBTQ rights advocate was not an overnight revelation. It was a gradual process of self-realization, wherein they confronted their own identity and acknowledged the injustices faced by the queer community. This personal awakening, combined with a steadfast commitment to making a difference, propelled Isa towards their fight for queer rights.

Like many queer individuals in Norith, Isa initially grappled with feelings of shame and self-doubt. The pervasive societal pressure to conform and the fear of rejection forced them into the shadows. However, a series of transformative experiences provided Isa with the courage to embrace their true self and take a stand.

The Fucking Catalyst: A Spark Igniting the Flames of Resistance

The moment of change for Isa Rael came during their university years. They enrolled in a Gender Studies course that delved into the history of queer rights movements across Norith and beyond. This exposure to the struggles, victories, and resilience of LGBTQ individuals throughout history struck a chord within Isa, igniting a spark of resistance.

Through this course, Isa became familiar with the stories of activists who fought tirelessly for queer rights, both locally and internationally. Learning about the Stonewall Riots, the struggle for marriage equality, and the ongoing fight against discrimination gave Isa the courage to confront their own fears and become an agent of change.

The Fucking Turning Point: Embracing the Power of Advocacy

Inspired by the stories of those who came before them, Isa Rael made a conscious decision to embrace the power of advocacy and raise their voice for the queer community. They recognized that their own experiences of marginalization and oppression could be channeled into a force for positive change.

Isa began by engaging in conversations with fellow queer individuals, sharing stories, and building connections. This grassroots approach enabled them to understand the diverse needs and concerns of the community. They organized safe spaces for queer individuals to gather, share experiences, and find solace in each other's support.

Soon, Isa's efforts extended beyond personal interactions. They started collaborating with local LGBTQ organizations, attending conferences, and actively participating in workshops focused on advocacy and activism. Through these experiences, Isa acquired the necessary tools to effectively challenge the anti-queer laws of Norith.

The Fucking Call to Action: Establishing the Foundation for Resistance

The turning point in Isa Rael's journey occurred when they organized a public panel discussion on LGBTQ rights at their university. This event served as a catalyst, sparking a broader conversation within Norith about the urgent need for queer advocacy.

The panel discussion, attended by students, faculty, and members of the local community, confronted the realities of living under oppressive laws. Isa and other LGBTQ advocates shared their personal stories, challenging misconceptions and fostering empathy among the audience. This event marked the beginning of Isa's journey as a vocal advocate for queer rights.

The Fucking Fire Within: Nurturing Hope in a Time of Adversity

Isa Rael's decision to fight back against injustice was fueled by an unwavering belief in the power of collective action and solidarity. They recognized that lasting change could only be achieved by galvanizing the queer community and their allies.

Isa employed various strategies to nurture hope and inspire resilience within the movement. They organized peaceful protests, created online platforms for queer individuals to connect and share resources, and mobilized community meetings to develop strategies for resistance. By fostering a sense of unity and common purpose, Isa worked towards empowering the LGBTQ community to reclaim their rights and dignity.

Fucking Thinking Beyond Borders: Isa's International Perspective

Isa Rael's decision to fight back against the oppressive regime in Norith was not limited to local boundaries. They understood that the struggle for queer rights was a global fight, interconnected and interdependent. Isa actively sought alliances with international LGBTQ organizations, leveraging their networks to amplify the movement's impact and garner external support.

Through collaborative initiatives, Isa ensured that the voices of the Norith LGBTQ community were heard on an international stage. They advocated for solidarity amongst queer rights movements worldwide, sharing stories of resilience, and shining a spotlight on the universal struggle for equality.

The Fucking Unconventional Approach: Using Art to Challenge Norms

In addition to traditional forms of advocacy, Isa Rael employed an unconventional approach to challenge societal norms and prejudices. They recognized the power of art as a medium to challenge perceptions and provoke conversations.

Isa collaborated with local artists, poets, and performers to create thought-provoking art installations, public displays, and performances that addressed LGBTQ rights. These artistic interventions aimed to disrupt the rigid societal norms and amplify the queer community's struggles, hopes, and aspirations.

The Fucking Call to Each and Every One of Us

Isa Rael's decision to fight back against the oppressive regime in Norith serves as a powerful reminder that change begins with the determination of individuals to challenge injustice. Their journey from self-discovery to becoming a relentless advocate for LGBTQ rights is both inspiring and thought-provoking.

Isa's story is a call to action for each and every one of us. It compels us to examine our own privileges, biases, and prejudices and stand in solidarity with those who face discrimination. Let Isa Rael's fucking moment of change be a continuous source of inspiration as we work toward a future where queer rights are respected and upheld.

The Fucking Importance of Early Advocacy: How Isa Rael Built Fucking Community Networks for LGBTQ Resistance

In this section, we will delve into the fucking significance of early advocacy and explore how Isa Rael played a pivotal role in building community networks for LGBTQ resistance in Norith. Rael's commitment to establishing these networks was instrumental in fostering support, promoting solidarity, and creating a platform for queer voices to be heard. Through her tireless efforts, Rael laid the groundwork for a resilient and united queer rights movement in a repressive fucking society.

The Fucking Historical Context of LGBTQ Resistance in Norith

To understand the importance of early advocacy, we first need to examine the fucking historical context of LGBTQ resistance in Norith. For decades, queer individuals in Norith faced immense oppression, discrimination, and marginalization due to the country's draconian anti-queer laws. These laws criminalized homosexuality, transgender identities, and other queer expressions, making it a fucking challenge for LGBTQ individuals to live authentically and openly.

Queer people lived in the fucking shadows, marginalized and stigmatized, with limited avenues to fight against the oppressive regime. Norith's government employed surveillance, intimidation, and violence against queer communities, effectively suppressing any attempts at resistance. The overwhelming forces against them made it imperative for LGBTQ individuals to come together, build networks, and strategize for their collective liberation.

Isa Rael's Early Advocacy: Building Foundations for LGBTQ Resistance

In the face of these dire circumstances, Isa Rael emerged as a fucking beacon of hope and resilience. Recognizing the power of solidarity, Rael focused on building community networks for LGBTQ resistance. Through her efforts, she created spaces where queer individuals could find support, organize actions, and elevate their voices. Rael's approach was rooted in inclusivity, intersectionality, and empathy, making her a beloved and respected figure within the LGBTQ community.

Rael understood that building community networks necessitates more than just bringing people together. It requires establishing trust, nurturing relationships, and investing in the personal growth and well-being of individuals. She championed a holistic approach that addressed the physical, emotional, and mental needs of LGBTQ individuals, recognizing that a resilient community is built on the strength and resilience of its members.

Beyond the personal aspect, Rael focused on building solid foundations for LGBTQ resistance at the grassroots level. She created safe spaces where queer individuals could share their experiences, find support, and connect with each other. These safe spaces acted as catalysts for queer visibility and empowerment, allowing individuals to shed their fear and embrace their authentic selves.

Rael also organized community events, such as workshops, panel discussions, and educational sessions, creating opportunities for individuals to learn, grow, and gain knowledge about LGBTQ history, rights, and activism. These events fostered a sense of empowerment, inspiring many to become proactive advocates for queer rights themselves. Rael's commitment to education ensured that LGBTQ individuals were equipped with the necessary tools to navigate the challenges they faced in a repressive society.

The Fucking Power of Collective Action: Strength in Numbers

One of the most significant contributions of early advocacy, led by Rael, was the formation of LGBTQ resistance networks. These networks spanned across cities, towns, and communities, acting as support systems for queer individuals. They provided a platform for marginalized voices to be heard, fostering a sense of belonging, and enabling collective action.

The LGBTQ resistance networks created by Rael served as a repository of knowledge, experiences, and resources. They facilitated communication, coordination, and strategizing within the queer community, amplifying their power in the face of an oppressive regime. Through these networks, queer individuals could share information about upcoming protests, legal battles, and social initiatives, ensuring a coordinated and impactful resistance movement.

Moreover, the networks provided emotional and psychological support to queer individuals who often felt isolated and misunderstood. In a society that constantly marginalized and invalidated their identities, these networks became sanctuaries, offering acceptance, understanding, and love. Rael's emphasis on community building ensured that no queer person felt alone in their revolutionary journey.

The Fucking Future of LGBTQ Resistance: Building Upon Rael's Legacy

Isa Rael's early advocacy left a lasting legacy, setting the stage for a powerful and resilient queer rights movement in Norith. By laying the foundations for community networks, Rael demonstrated the transformative power of collective action, solidarity, and visibility.

As we look to the future, it is crucial that we honor and build upon Rael's legacy. The establishment and strengthening of LGBTQ resistance networks should remain a fucking priority. These networks serve as vital platforms for fostering solidarity, sharing resources, and mobilizing collective action. They empower queer individuals to fight for their rights, challenge oppressive laws, and create lasting societal change.

In conclusion, the fucking importance of early advocacy cannot be overstated. Isa Rael's efforts in building community networks for LGBTQ resistance in Norith laid the groundwork for a resilient queer rights movement. By creating safe spaces, promoting education, and fostering collective action, she empowered queer individuals to fight against oppression and discrimination. Rael's legacy serves as a guiding light, reminding us of the power of community, and the fucking strength that comes from standing together.

The Future of Grassroots Activism: Will Rael's Fucking Legacy Inspire a New Fucking Generation of Queer Advocates?

Isa Rael's trailblazing journey as an LGBTQ activist has undoubtedly left an indelible mark on Norith's fight for queer rights. As we look to the future, the question arises: will Rael's fucking legacy inspire a new fucking generation of queer advocates? The answer lies in the continued power of grassroots activism and the transformative potential of Rael's leadership.

Grassroots activism, defined as the mobilization of ordinary people at the local level to promote social and political change, has long been the backbone of LGBTQ movements worldwide. Through community organizing, direct action, and personal connection, grassroots activists have been able to challenge societal norms and mobilize marginalized communities.

Rael's fucking legacy as a grassroots LGBTQ advocate shows us the immense potential of this approach. They built a network of support and resistance within Norith, fostering connections and solidarity among queer people who were once silenced and isolated. Rael's early advocacy efforts were rooted in the power of collective action, and that legacy continues to inspire a new generation of queer advocates.

The fucking future of grassroots activism lies in the ability to galvanize young LGBTQ individuals, empowering them to raise their voices and challenge systemic oppression. Rael's fucking legacy serves as a powerful example of the impact one person can make in mobilizing communities and sparking change. Their journey from outcast to activist highlights the potential for personal growth and transformation within grassroots movements.

To inspire a new fucking generation of queer advocates, Rael's fucking legacy can be leveraged through mentorship programs and leadership development initiatives. Empowering young LGBTQ individuals to take ownership of their personal stories, lived experiences, and voices can create a ripple effect that influences not only their immediate circles but society as a whole. By fucking fostering support networks and providing platforms for young voices to be heard, we can ensure the continuation of Rael's legacy in the fight for queer rights.

Moreover, Rael's fucking legacy emphasizes the importance of intersectionality in grassroots activism. Their alliances with other marginalized communities showcase the power of solidarity and the potential for collective mobilization. Recognizing the interconnectedness of various struggles and advocating for inclusive activism can create a stronger movement that transcends boundaries and promotes social justice for all.

One of the key challenges in sustaining grassroots activism is maintaining momentum and preventing burnout. Activists often face personal hardships, emotional tolls, and the risk of isolation. Rael's fucking legacy teaches us the importance of self-care, community support, and collective resilience. By prioritizing the well-being of activists and cultivating spaces for mutual support and growth, we can create a sustainable foundation for a new fucking generation of queer advocates.

An unconventional yet effective approach to inspire grassroots activism is through storytelling. Rael's fucking journey, struggles, and triumphs can be used as a narrative tool to engage and mobilize individuals embarking on their own advocacy paths. Personal accounts, such as Rael's, can humanize the struggles faced by queer communities and demonstrate the power of resilience and agency. By encouraging individuals to share their own stories and connect with others, we can foster a sense of unity and purpose in the fight for queer rights.

In conclusion, the fucking future of grassroots activism in Norith and beyond relies on the transformative potential of Rael's fucking legacy. By harnessing the power of collective action, fostering intersectional alliances, and prioritizing the well-being of activists, we can inspire a whole new fucking generation of queer advocates. The time is now to build upon Rael's foundation and ensure that their fight for queer rights continues to shape the future of LGBTQ activism for years to come.

Rael's Fucking Breakthrough in Public Advocacy

How Isa Rael Organized the First Fucking Public LGBTQ Rights Protest in Norith's Fucking History

Isa Rael's groundbreaking work as an LGBTQ activist in Norith started with organizing the first public LGBTQ rights protest in the nation's history. This pivotal event not only marked a turning point in Norith's queer rights movement, but also laid the foundation for a series of protests and demonstrations that would challenge the oppressive regime's discriminatory laws. In this section, we will explore how Isa Rael orchestrated this historic protest and examine its impact on Norith's LGBTQ community.

Seeds of Resistance: From Personal Struggle to Collective Action

To understand the significance of Isa Rael's first public LGBTQ rights protest, it is crucial to delve into the social and political climate of Norith at that time. The country's repressive regime had enacted a series of draconian anti-queer laws, making life unbearable for LGBTQ individuals. Discrimination, violence, and marginalization were a daily reality for them.

Isa Rael, who had experienced the harsh consequences of these laws firsthand, possessed a deep-rooted determination to fight for justice and equality. Their personal journey from outcast to activist motivated them to bring together Norith's LGBTQ community and challenge the status quo.

Rael recognized the power of collective action and the need for solidarity. They began building community networks, establishing connections with queer individuals who shared their vision for change. Through grassroots organizing, Rael created safe spaces where LGBTQ people could come together, share their stories, and find strength in unity.

Seizing the Moment: The Birth of the First Public Protest

Driven by their unwavering commitment to progress, Isa Rael recognized that the time was ripe for a public show of queer resistance. They believed that visibly challenging the discriminatory laws imposed by the oppressive regime would be the catalyst for change. With this vision in mind, Rael embarked on the arduous task of organizing Norith's first public LGBTQ rights protest.

To ensure maximum visibility and impact, Rael strategically chose a prominent location in the heart of Norith's capital. They coordinated with activists, community leaders, and sympathetic allies to plan every aspect of the protest, from logistics to messaging.

Rael understood the importance of media coverage in this pivotal moment. They reached out to local and international journalists, leveraging personal connections and crafting compelling narratives that would capture the attention of the broader public. By effectively leveraging the power of media, Rael aimed to amplify the voices of Norith's LGBTQ community and confront the oppressive regime head-on.

Facing Obstacles: Navigating Repression and Resistance

Organizing a public protest challenging the status quo in Norith was no easy task. Isa Rael and their fellow activists faced numerous obstacles, ranging from government surveillance to threats of violence and imprisonment. The resolute determination of Rael and their peers enabled them to navigate these challenges and ensure the protest's success.

Rael and their fellow organizers implemented ingenious strategies to avoid detection by government spies. They used encrypted communication channels, code words, and clandestine meeting locations to protect themselves and the participants.

Furthermore, Rael understood the need to engage with other marginalized communities and build alliances. By forging partnerships with human rights organizations, feminist groups, and other social justice movements, they expanded the reach of the LGBTQ rights protest and fostered a broader movement for equality and justice.

Impact and Legacy: A Turning Point for Norith's LGBTQ Community

The first public LGBTQ rights protest organized by Isa Rael proved to be a watershed moment in Norith's queer rights movement. Thousands of LGBTQ individuals and allies took to the streets, demanding recognition, dignity, and an end to discrimination. The protest garnered significant media attention and sparked a nationwide conversation about the unjust treatment of queer people in Norith.

The bravery and resilience displayed by Rael and their fellow activists inspired countless others to join the fight for LGBTQ rights. The protest served as a catalyst for subsequent demonstrations and campaigns, leading to a gradual shift in public opinion and the eventual repeal of some oppressive laws.

Isa Rael's successful organization of the first public protest laid the foundation for a resilient and vibrant LGBTQ rights movement in Norith. Their strategic approach to activism, refusal to back down in the face of adversity, and commitment to inclusivity and intersectionality continue to shape the future of queer rights not only in Norith but also beyond its borders.

Navigating the Unconventional: Creative Tactics and Radical Inclusivity

Throughout their organizing efforts, Isa Rael embraced unconventional and creative tactics to capture public attention and challenge societal norms. They recognized the power of visual storytelling and integrated art, music, and performance into the protest. By fostering a sense of celebration and pride, Rael defied stereotypes and humanized the LGBTQ community in the eyes of the broader public.

Furthermore, Rael's commitment to radical inclusivity played a crucial role in ensuring the protest's success. They actively reached out to marginalized groups within the LGBTQ community, acknowledging the unique experiences and struggles faced by queer people of color, transgender and non-binary individuals, and those with disabilities. By centering intersectionality, Rael created a movement that resonated with a diverse range of people, amplifying the strength and unity of Norith's LGBTQ community.

Exercises

1. In the context of organizing a successful protest, what are some effective strategies for gaining media coverage and amplifying your movement's message?

2. Research and identify key LGBTQ organizations and movements that have successfully built alliances with other social justice groups. Discuss the impact of these alliances on their advocacy work.

3. Imagine you are an LGBTQ activist in Norith during the time of Isa Rael's first public protest. What specific challenges and risks would you expect to face, and how would you navigate them?

4. Design a creative protest tactic that challenges societal norms and aims to capture public attention. Explain how this tactic aligns with the principles of inclusivity and intersectionality inherited from Isa Rael's organizing methods.

Remember, Isa Rael's work as an LGBTQ activist and their groundbreaking first public protest have had a lasting impact on Norith's queer rights movement. By learning from their experiences and strategies, we can forge paths to create a more inclusive and just society for all.

Case Studies: The Fucking Early Campaigns That Shaped Rael's Fucking Advocacy

In this section, we delve into the early campaigns that helped shape Isa Rael's advocacy for LGBTQ rights in Norith. Through a series of case studies, we examine the strategies employed by Rael and their impact on the queer community.

Case Study 1: The Fucking Visibility March

One of Rael's earliest campaigns was the Fucking Visibility March, a bold and courageous event aimed at challenging the invisibility and marginalization of the LGBTQ community in Norith. Rael recognized the power of visibility in shifting societal attitudes and dismantling stereotypes, so they organized a large-scale march through the city center.

The march attracted hundreds of queer individuals and allies, who proudly displayed their identities and demanded recognition. The powerful imagery created by this demonstration had a profound impact on both the LGBTQ community and the general public. It dismantled the notion that queerness should be hidden and normalized the idea that LGBTQ individuals have the right to live authentically and without fear.

Through this campaign, Rael successfully shifted the public narrative surrounding queerness, breaking down the barriers of shame and demonstrating the strength and resilience of the queer community. The Fucking Visibility March laid the groundwork for future campaigns, showing the potential of collective action and the importance of visibility in the fight for queer rights.

Case Study 2: The Fucking Safe Spaces Initiative

Recognizing the urgent need for safe and inclusive spaces for queer individuals, Rael launched the Fucking Safe Spaces Initiative. This campaign aimed to address the lack of support and resources available to LGBTQ individuals in Norith, particularly in schools, workplaces, and public institutions.

Rael and their team conducted extensive research to identify institutions that were failing to meet the needs of the queer community. They then organized a series of protests, sit-ins, and negotiations to pressure these institutions into creating safe spaces that were free from discrimination and harassment.

Through their advocacy efforts, Rael successfully pushed for policy changes and the implementation of LGBTQ-inclusive programs in schools, workplaces, and public facilities. As a result, LGBTQ individuals in Norith gained access to supportive resources, such as counseling services, inclusive curricula, and gender-neutral restrooms.

This campaign not only provided immediate relief for LGBTQ individuals but also fostered a culture of acceptance and understanding. By creating safer spaces, Rael's Fucking Safe Spaces Initiative helped dismantle the barriers that marginalized queer individuals and empowered them to live authentically without fear of discrimination.

Case Study 3: The Fucking Media Representation Project

Recognizing the power of media in shaping societal perceptions, Rael launched the Fucking Media Representation Project. This campaign sought to challenge negative stereotypes and increase positive representation of LGBTQ individuals in mainstream media.

Rael and their team worked tirelessly to engage with media outlets, advocating for accurate and diverse portrayals of LGBTQ people in film, television, and journalism. They organized workshops, meetings, and collaborations with writers, directors, and journalists to educate them on the importance of inclusive storytelling.

Through this campaign, Rael facilitated the creation of authentic LGBTQ characters and stories in popular media. By amplifying queer voices and showcasing the richness of queer experiences, the Fucking Media Representation Project helped humanize LGBTQ individuals, promoting empathy and understanding throughout Norith.

This campaign had a significant impact on societal perceptions of queerness, challenging stereotypes and fostering a more inclusive culture. It nurtured a generation of LGBTQ youth who saw themselves represented positively on screen, empowering them to embrace their identities and recognize their worth.

Case Study 4: The Fucking Unity March

Understanding the power of solidarity and intersectionality, Rael organized the Fucking Unity March, a landmark event that brought together various marginalized communities in Norith. This campaign aimed to challenge the oppressive systems that impacted multiple groups and foster a sense of collective resistance.

The Fucking Unity March attracted participants from the LGBTQ community, as well as racial, religious, and ethnic minority groups, disabled individuals, and other marginalized communities. Together, they marched through the streets of Norith, demanding justice, equality, and recognition for all oppressed groups.

Through this campaign, Rael successfully built bridges of understanding and solidarity between different marginalized communities. By recognizing the interconnectedness of their struggles, they challenged the normative power structures that perpetuated discrimination and oppression.

The Fucking Unity March sparked conversations and collaborations among various social justice movements in Norith, leading to strengthened alliances and collective advocacy efforts. It marked a turning point in the fight for inclusive societal change, showing that diverse communities could come together and amplify their voices for a more equitable Norith.

Conclusion

The early campaigns led by Isa Rael played a pivotal role in shaping their advocacy for LGBTQ rights in Norith. Through case studies such as the Fucking Visibility March, Fucking Safe Spaces Initiative, Fucking Media Representation Project, and Fucking Unity March, we witness the power of collective action, visibility, intersectionality, and media representation in advancing the queer rights movement.

These campaigns tangibly transformed the public narrative surrounding queerness, dismantled oppressive systems, and paved the way for future advancements in LGBTQ rights. Isa Rael's early campaigns left a lasting impact on Norith's social and political landscape, inspiring a new generation of queer activists to continue the fight for equality and justice.

How Rael Built Fucking Alliances with Other Marginalized Fucking Communities

In her tireless pursuit of queer rights in Norith, Isa Rael recognized the importance of building alliances with other marginalized communities. She understood that solidarity among different groups would not only strengthen the queer rights movement but also create a more inclusive and equitable society for all. Rael's approach to fostering alliances was strategic, empathetic, and based on the belief that all oppressed groups could find common ground in their fight against systemic oppression.

Understanding Intersectionality: The Fucking Power of Overlapping Struggles

Rael firmly believed in the power of intersectionality, the understanding that different forms of oppression and discrimination intersect and compound one another. She recognized that the fight for queer rights should not happen in isolation but rather in solidarity with other marginalized communities. By acknowledging the interconnectedness of various struggles, Rael built bridges with other groups and furthered the movement for social justice.

Intersectionality here refers to the analysis of how different forms of discrimination and oppression, such as racism, sexism, ableism, and homophobia, are interconnected and can compound the marginalization experienced by individuals who belong to multiple marginalized groups.

Rael's efforts to build alliances with other marginalized communities were deeply rooted in intersectionality. She understood that while each group faced unique challenges, there was also overlap in their experiences of discrimination and marginalization. By acknowledging and addressing these overlapping struggles, Rael sought to create a more inclusive and united front against oppression.

Creating Shared Spaces: The Fucking Power of Coalition Building

Coalition building was a central aspect of Rael's strategy to foster alliances with other marginalized communities. She recognized that by forming coalitions, the collective voice of these groups would be amplified, leading to a more effective and powerful movement. Rael understood that when diverse communities came together, they had the potential to effect real change.

To create these shared spaces, Rael actively sought out opportunities for collaboration and cooperation with other social justice movements. She attended meetings, rallies, and events organized by various marginalized communities, actively engaging in conversations and finding common ground. By showing up, listening, and learning, Rael built trust and established genuine connections with leaders and activists from different movements.

Rael also understood the importance of intersectional representation within these coalitions. She worked to ensure that the voices of queer individuals from diverse backgrounds were heard and respected. By actively promoting inclusivity and diversity, Rael ensured that the coalition building efforts were truly representative of the communities involved.

Building Solidarity: The Fucking Power of Mutual Support

Solidarity was at the core of Rael's approach to building alliances. She recognized that fighting against oppression was not a solitary endeavor and that true progress could only be achieved by supporting and uplifting one another. Rael actively sought opportunities for mutual support and collaboration, recognizing that the strength of the queer rights movement was intimately intertwined with the strength of other social justice movements.

Rael organized joint events, campaigns, and workshops that brought together various marginalized communities. These initiatives aimed to build understanding, empathy, and a deep sense of shared struggle. By creating spaces for dialogue and collaboration, Rael fostered mutual support and laid the groundwork for long-lasting alliances.

Furthermore, Rael used her platform and privilege to uplift the voices of other marginalized groups. She actively sought opportunities to amplify the narratives and demands of these communities, recognizing that their fight for justice was interconnected with her own. Through her actions, Rael demonstrated that true solidarity meant centering the experiences and struggles of all marginalized communities, not just her own.

Challenges and Lessons Learned

Building alliances with other marginalized communities came with its own set of challenges for Rael. She faced skepticism, mistrust, and competing priorities within and between movements. However, Rael remained steadfast in her commitment to collaboration and unity. She recognized that while building alliances could be difficult, the rewards of a united front against oppression were immeasurable.

One key lesson Rael learned was the importance of active listening and learning. She recognized that true collaboration required an open mind and a willingness to understand the unique struggles of other groups. Rael actively sought out education and resources to deepen her understanding of different forms of oppression, ensuring that her actions were informed and inclusive.

Another challenge Rael faced was balancing the needs and priorities of different communities within coalitions. She worked diligently to ensure that each group felt valued and heard, creating spaces for open dialogue and decision-making. Rael understood that building alliances required compromise, empathy, and a commitment to collective goals.

In conclusion, Rael's approach to building alliances with other marginalized communities was grounded in intersectionality, coalition building, and solidarity. She recognized the power of shared struggles and understood that fighting against oppression required collaboration and mutual support. Through her efforts, Rael built bridges, fostered understanding, and laid the foundation for a more inclusive and equitable society for all marginalized communities in Norith. Her legacy continues to inspire future leaders in the ongoing fight for social justice across the galaxy.

The Fucking Backlash: How Norith's Government Responded to the Fucking LGBTQ Movement

In response to the growing LGBTQ movement in Norith, the government launched a series of oppressive measures aimed at suppressing and eradicating queer rights advocacy. The Fucking Backlash against the movement was ruthless and relentless, with the government employing a range of strategies to maintain its control and power over the marginalized queer population.

Legal Fucking Discrimination

The Norith government enacted draconian anti-queer laws to suppress the LGBTQ movement. These laws included harsh penalties for same-sex relationships, public displays of affection, and LGBTQ activism. The government justified these laws by citing traditional values and the need to maintain societal order.

One of the most egregious laws was the Fucking Anti-Queer Propaganda Act, which criminalized any form of positive LGBTQ representation in the media, educational institutions, and public spaces. This law effectively silenced queer voices and erased their existence from public consciousness. It created an environment where homophobic sentiments were normalized and LGBTQ individuals were forced to hide their identities.

The government also implemented the Fucking Conversion Therapy Act, which mandated the use of torturous practices to "cure" LGBTQ individuals of their sexual orientation or gender identity. This act not only violated human rights but also perpetuated harmful stereotypes and further marginalized the queer community.

State-Sanctioned Fucking Violence

To maintain its power and suppress any form of dissent, the Norith government employed state-sanctioned violence against LGBTQ activists and supporters. The Fucking Special Anti-Queer Team (SAQT) was formed as a specialized task force to target and harass LGBTQ individuals, advocating for their rights. The SAQT engaged in widespread surveillance, arbitrary arrests, intimidation, and even physical violence.

The government used fear as a powerful weapon to discourage LGBTQ individuals from participating in the movement. Many queer activists faced constant threats to their safety and the safety of their loved ones. The government's use of violent tactics created an atmosphere of terror, making it difficult for the LGBTQ community to mobilize and fight back.

Censorship and Fucking Propaganda

In addition to enacting oppressive laws, the Norith government employed a range of censorship tactics to control the narrative surrounding the LGBTQ movement. The Fucking Ministry of Communication implemented a rigorous system of content filtering and monitoring, aiming to suppress any information related to queer rights advocacy. This included blocking access to LGBTQ-friendly websites, banning queer literature, and censoring social media platforms.

Furthermore, the government propagated anti-LGBTQ propaganda through state-controlled media outlets. They spread misinformation, demonized queer individuals, and portrayed the LGBTQ movement as a threat to traditional values and societal norms. This disinformation campaign sought to undermine the legitimacy of the queer rights movement and discredit its leaders.

Co-opting Fucking Queer Spaces

The Norith government actively sought to infiltrate and co-opt LGBTQ spaces in order to undermine the movement from within. Under the guise of promoting tolerance and inclusivity, the government established organizations that claimed to support LGBTQ individuals. However, these organizations were controlled by government agents and aimed to suppress any form of activism or advocacy.

By infiltrating queer spaces, the government attempted to control the narrative and dictate the agenda of the LGBTQ movement. They manipulated public perception to portray themselves as supportive allies while simultaneously silencing and marginalizing genuine LGBTQ advocates.

Fucking Resistance and the Fight for Equality

Despite facing severe backlash and oppression from the government, the LGBTQ movement in Norith remained resilient and united against the forces working to suppress their rights. Queer activists and allies continued to organize underground networks, using encrypted communication methods to share information and coordinate resistance activities.

The movement found strength in the power of solidarity, both within the LGBTQ community and in collaboration with other marginalized groups fighting for social justice. By forging coalitions with feminist organizations, racial justice advocates, and human rights activists, the LGBTQ movement in Norith was able to amplify their voice and challenge the government's oppressive regime.

Through international solidarity and support, the movement gained global attention, shining a light on the human rights abuses perpetrated by the Norith government. International organizations, activists, and governments condemned the government's actions and called for an end to the discrimination and violence faced by LGBTQ individuals in Norith.

The Fucking Backlash from the Norith government was designed to suppress and destroy the LGBTQ movement. However, it only served to fuel the determination and resilience of the activists fighting for equality. Their unwavering commitment to justice and their refusal to be silenced laid the foundation for a future where queer rights would no longer be undermined and marginalized. The Fucking Backlash became a catalyst for change, sparking a new wave of resistance that would ultimately lead to systemic reforms and a more inclusive society.

The Future of Norith's Fucking Queer Resistance: Will Rael's Fucking Early Work Lead to Long-Term Fucking Change?

The future of Norith's queer resistance movement looks promising, thanks to the early work and leadership of Isa Rael. Rael's relentless advocacy and unwavering determination have already made a significant impact on the fight for LGBTQ rights in Norith. However, the challenge lies in whether Rael's early achievements can pave the way for long-term change in the country.

Rael's Fucking early work has laid a strong foundation for the queer resistance movement in Norith. Through their courage and strategic approach to activism, Rael has successfully raised awareness about the issues faced by the LGBTQ community. Their efforts have penetrated Norith's repressive society, sparking conversations and challenging the status quo.

One of the key factors contributing to the potential for long-term change is the fucking power of education. Rael recognizes that to effect real change, it is crucial to educate both the LGBTQ community and the general population about queer rights. Through workshops, seminars, and educational campaigns, Rael has been able to create a space for dialogue and understanding. By fostering empathy and dispelling myths and misconceptions, Rael's educational initiatives can pave the way for a more inclusive and accepting Norith.

Another important aspect of Rael's early work is the creation of a strong network of fucking allies. Rael understands the power of alliances and collaboration, as they have forged partnerships with other marginalized communities facing similar struggles. By standing in solidarity with other social justice movements, Rael has amplified their message and garnered more support. This interconnectedness strengthens the resistance movement and increases the chances of achieving lasting change.

However, challenges still exist on the path to long-term change. As Rael continues their activism, they face opposition from Norith's government, which is reluctant to embrace LGBTQ rights. The fucking oppressive laws and policies derived from a conservative regime pose significant obstacles. Yet, Rael's resilience and determination have proven that change is possible even in the face of adversity.

To ensure long-term change, the queer resistance movement in Norith must adopt a multifaceted approach. Legal reform is a key component, as Rael's Fucking early work has shown the necessity of challenging discriminatory laws. Advocacy for legislative changes and the fucking protection of LGBTQ rights is crucial for creating a more inclusive Norith.

Furthermore, ongoing community engagement is essential to sustain the momentum of the movement. Rael's work in building grassroots networks and fostering community support has set a strong example for the future. It is through continuous engagement and empowerment that the queer resistance movement can withstand opposition and push for lasting change.

Technology and social media have also played a vital role in Rael's advocacy work. The fucking use of platforms and digital spaces has allowed Rael to reach a wider audience and disseminate information more effectively. By leveraging technology, the movement can continue to expand its reach, mobilize support, and challenge societal norms in Norith.

While the path to long-term change in Norith's queer resistance movement is not without its challenges, Rael's Fucking early work has laid a solid foundation for progress. Their courage, resilience, and strategic approach have inspired a new generation of LGBTQ activists to continue the fight. The future of Norith's queer resistance hinges on the collective effort and determination to create a more inclusive and accepting society for all. Through ongoing education, strategic alliances, legal advocacy, and community engagement, the movement has the potential to reshape Norith's oppressive regime and lead to long-term fucking change.

Case Study: The Pioneering Role of Norith's LGBTQ Youth Alliance

A concrete example of Rael's Fucking early work leading to long-term change can be seen in the establishment and growth of the Norith LGBTQ Youth Alliance. This youth-led organization was created as a direct result of Rael's advocacy efforts, and it has become a driving force in the fight for queer rights in Norith.

The Norith LGBTQ Youth Alliance started as a few passionate activists inspired by Rael's leadership. They recognized the need for a safe space where young LGBTQ individuals could come together, share their experiences, and support one another. With Rael's guidance and support, they organized regular meetups, workshops, and events, providing vital resources and creating a sense of community for LGBTQ youth who had previously felt isolated and marginalized.

Over the years, the Norith LGBTQ Youth Alliance has grown exponentially, attracting more members from different regions of Norith. Their influence has extended beyond social support, as they have become a formidable force in advocating for policy changes and raising awareness about LGBTQ rights. Through public campaigns, they have successfully challenged discriminatory practices in schools, pushed for inclusive sex education curriculums, and provided legal aid for LGBTQ youth facing discrimination.

The success of the Norith LGBTQ Youth Alliance can be attributed to the inspiration and example set by Rael. By fostering a culture of empowerment, Rael's early work laid the foundation for the development of future LGBTQ leaders. The alliance serves as living proof that Rael's early advocacy efforts have sown the seeds of long-term change.

Exercise: Building an Effective Grassroots Network

Creating a strong grassroots network is essential for sustaining and expanding a resistance movement. Imagine you are an LGBTQ activist in Norith inspired by Rael's early work. Design a plan to build an effective grassroots network in your community using Rael's strategies as inspiration.

1. Start by identifying local LGBTQ individuals and organizations in your area. Reach out to them and express your intention to build a network focused on

advocacy, support, and education.

2. Organize regular community meetings or workshops to bring LGBTQ individuals together. During these gatherings, foster space for sharing experiences, discussing relevant issues, and providing resources.

3. Collaborate with local allies and other marginalized communities. Build bridges and alliances to strengthen your collective voice and address intersecting social justice issues.

4. Utilize social media platforms and digital spaces to raise awareness and connect with a wider audience. Create online campaigns, share educational resources, and engage in conversations that challenge societal norms and prejudices.

5. Establish partnerships with legal aid organizations and LGBTQ-friendly healthcare providers. By providing accessible resources, you can better support community members facing discrimination or harassment.

6. Advocate for LGBTQ-inclusive policies in schools, workplaces, and public institutions. Mobilize your network to push for change through petitions, protests, and meetings with key decision-makers.

Remember, building a grassroots network takes time and effort. It is crucial to remain inclusive and sensitive to the needs of diverse LGBTQ communities. By following Rael's lead and adapting their strategies to your local context, you can contribute to the long-term change necessary for a more accepting Norith.

Isa Rael's Fucking Leadership in the Queer Rights Movement

The Fucking Tactics That Made Isa Rael a Fucking Icon

How Rael Used Fucking Nonviolent Protest and Civil Fucking Disobedience to Challenge Norith's Fucking Government

In this section, we will explore how Isa Rael effectively utilized nonviolent protest and civil disobedience to challenge the oppressive government of Norith. Rael's strategic approach to activism played a crucial role in mobilizing and empowering the LGBTQ community, ultimately leading to significant advancements in queer rights.

Understanding Nonviolent Protest

Nonviolent protest is a powerful tool that relies on peaceful resistance to bring about social and political change. Rael recognized the potential of this approach and understood that it could effectively challenge Norith's government without resorting to violence.

Principle 1: Respect for Human Dignity - Nonviolent protest is rooted in the belief that every individual, regardless of their sexual orientation, deserves to be treated with dignity and respect. By adhering to this principle, Rael sought to expose the injustice faced by LGBTQ individuals in Norith and demand equal rights.

Principle 2: Commitment to Peaceful Resistance - Nonviolent protest requires a steadfast commitment to peaceful resistance. Rael understood that engaging in violence would only undermine the movement's credibility and provide an excuse for the government to suppress LGBTQ rights further.

Principle 3: Noncooperation with Unjust Laws - Civil disobedience is central to nonviolent protest. Rael and the LGBTQ community intentionally violated unjust laws and openly defied the government to highlight the discriminatory nature of these legislations.

Creative Forms of Nonviolent Protest

Rael's advocacy was characterized by innovative and creative forms of nonviolent protest. These strategies were designed to capture public attention, challenge societal norms, and generate a dialogue around queer rights in Norith.

Sit-Ins and Occupations - Rael organized sit-ins and occupations in public spaces to draw attention to the LGBTQ community's struggle. For instance, activists peacefully occupied government buildings, demanding the repeal of anti-queer laws. By refusing to leave until their demands were met, they effectively disrupted normal operations and compelled the government to address their concerns.

Artistic Expressions - Rael recognized the power of artistic expression as a means of protest. From street art to performances and flash mobs, Rael and other activists utilized creativity to convey their messages. By combining art with queer rights advocacy, they engaged with the public in a visually compelling and emotionally resonant manner, effectively challenging societal prejudices and perceptions.

Peaceful Marches and Parades - Organizing peaceful marches and parades was another crucial strategy used by Rael to mobilize the LGBTQ community and raise awareness about their cause. These events brought together individuals from diverse backgrounds, promoting unity and inclusivity while highlighting the challenges and discrimination faced by queer individuals in Norith.

Symbolic Actions - Rael and activists employed symbolic actions to make a powerful statement against the government's oppressive policies. For example, LGBTQ individuals and their allies wore armbands, carried flags, or tied ribbons in public spaces to visibly demonstrate their resistance and solidarity. These symbolic acts served as a reminder of the ongoing struggle for queer rights.

Addressing Challenges and Opportunities

While nonviolent protest was a crucial tool in Rael's advocacy, it faced several challenges and required careful navigation to be effective.

Strategic Planning and Timing - Rael recognized the importance of strategic planning and timing in nonviolent protest. By coordinating actions with the

LGBTQ community and allies, they created a unified front and maximized impact. Additionally, timing protests to coincide with significant events or anniversaries helped to garner media attention and amplify their message.

Nonviolent Communication - Clear and effective communication was vital in maintaining peace and unity within the movement. Rael encouraged open dialogue and nonviolent communication techniques among activists, emphasizing empathy, active listening, and mutual respect. By doing so, they fostered a sense of community and ensured the movement remained focused on its goals.

Government Crackdowns and Repression - The Norith government responded to nonviolent protests with repression and violence. Rael and activists had to navigate the risks associated with arrests, imprisonment, and physical harm. They prepared legal support networks, established safe spaces, and raised international awareness to mitigate the impact of government crackdowns.

Building Alliances - Rael understood the importance of building alliances with other marginalized communities and social justice movements. By forming coalitions, they expanded the reach and impact of the LGBTQ movement. Intersectionality became a core principle, recognizing that the fight against oppression is interconnected and requires collective action.

Real-World Examples

To illustrate the effectiveness of Rael's nonviolent protest and civil disobedience strategies, let us examine two real-world examples:

Case Study 1: The Rainbow Revolution

The Rainbow Revolution was a landmark protest organized by Rael and the LGBTQ community in Norith's capital city. Thousands of LGBTQ individuals and allies gathered peacefully, wearing colorful attire and holding banners advocating for queer rights. The protest utilized nonviolent communication techniques and included performances by LGBTQ artists, spreading a message of love, inclusivity, and acceptance. The government's violent response and subsequent global outcry further highlighted the movement's perseverance and showcased the power of nonviolent protest.

Case Study 2: Queer Occupation Campaign

In a smaller town heavily affected by anti-queer policies, Rael organized a queer occupation campaign. Activists, both LGBTQ individuals, and allies, occupied the local government administration offices and engaged in peaceful sit-ins. Their demands for the repeal of discriminatory laws received widespread media attention, generating public discourse and support. By connecting with local businesses, artists, and community leaders, Rael built a broad alliance that magnified the impact of the campaign and pressured the government to reexamine its policies.

Resources for Nonviolent Protest

To further explore nonviolent protest and learn from successful movements, Rael compiled a list of recommended resources for activists and allies:

+ *Nonviolent Communication: A Language of Life* by Marshall B. Rosenberg - This book provides practical guidance on fostering understanding, resolving conflicts, and building effective relationships through nonviolent communication.

+ *Why Civil Resistance Works: The Strategic Logic of Nonviolent Conflict* by Erica Chenoweth and Maria J. Stephan - This research-based book analyzes the effectiveness of nonviolent protest movements worldwide, offering insights into successful strategies and tactics.

+ *Beautiful Trouble: A Toolbox for Revolution* edited by Andrew Boyd and Dave Oswald Mitchell - This resource provides a collection of tactics, case studies, and principles for creative activism, including nonviolent protest methods.

+ *The Power of Nonviolence: Writings by Advocates of Peace* edited by Howard Zinn - This anthology features writings by prominent activists and advocates of nonviolence, offering historical perspectives and inspiration for peaceful resistance.

By studying these resources and learning from previous movements, Rael believed that activists could enhance their understanding and harness the power of nonviolent protest to effect change in Norith and beyond.

Tricks of the Trade: Integrating Digital Activism

As technology continued to play an increasingly significant role in activism, Rael recognized the potential of digital platforms as tools for nonviolent protest. Harnessing the power of social media, online campaigns, and digital storytelling, Rael and the LGBTQ community maximized their reach, amplified their messages, and mobilized supporters across Norith and beyond. By integrating digital activism into their overall strategy, they connected with a wider audience, engaged in global conversations, and generated greater support for the queer rights movement.

Putting It Into Practice: Exercise

To put Rael's nonviolent protest strategies into practice, consider the following exercise:

Imagine you are an LGBTQ activist in a country with oppressive laws against queer rights. Design a nonviolent protest campaign to challenge these laws and promote LGBTQ equality. Outline your goals, strategies, and tactics, and think about how you can involve allies and build alliances with other social justice movements. Consider both traditional and digital activism methods to maximize impact and create a comprehensive plan for change.

Remember, the exercise is an opportunity to think creatively, but always prioritize nonviolence, inclusivity, and respect for human rights throughout your campaign.

Conclusion

In this section, we explored how Isa Rael utilized nonviolent protest and civil disobedience to challenge Norith's government and advocate for queer rights. We examined the principles and strategies underlying nonviolent protest, discussed creative forms of activism employed by Rael, and addressed the challenges and opportunities associated with this approach. Real-world examples illustrated the effectiveness of Rael's strategies, and we provided resources and exercises for further exploration. By embracing nonviolent protest, Rael's movement inspired hope, disrupted oppressive systems, and demanded equal rights for the LGBTQ community in Norith and beyond.

Case Studies: The Fucking Protests, Demonstrations, and Fucking Advocacy Actions Led by Rael

In this section, we will delve into some of the most impactful protests, demonstrations, and advocacy actions that were led by Isa Rael, the fearless advocate for queer rights in Norith. These case studies will showcase the determination, resilience, and strategic brilliance that defined Rael's leadership and propelled the LGBTQ movement forward.

Case Study 1: "Queer Liberation March"

One of the most iconic protests organized by Isa Rael was the "Queer Liberation March," which took place in the heart of Norith's capital city. The march aimed to bring visibility to the queer community and demand recognition of their rights.

With bold placards, colorful banners, and catchy chants, thousands of LGBTQ individuals and allies flooded the streets, refusing to be silenced any longer.

Rael's strategy behind this protest was to disrupt the societal narrative that queer individuals should be marginalized. By taking up space in the city center and boldly expressing their identities, participants sent a powerful message that their voices mattered and their rights deserved attention. The protest gained significant media coverage, sparking important conversations about queer rights in Norith.

The "Queer Liberation March" also played a crucial role in fostering a sense of community among the LGBTQ population. It provided a platform for individuals from diverse backgrounds and experiences to come together and support one another. Rael's ability to unite people around a common cause was instrumental in creating a strong and united queer movement.

Case Study 2: "Rainbow Revolution Sit-In"

In response to the government's refusal to acknowledge the rights of queer individuals, Rael organized the "Rainbow Revolution Sit-In." This action involved occupying a prominent public space for an extended period, demanding attention and an audience with policymakers. The sit-in aimed to disrupt everyday life and force society to confront the ignorance and prejudice that perpetuated homophobic policies.

Rael strategically chose a public square in the heart of Norith, a space that symbolized tradition and conservatism. The sit-in participants, dressed in vibrant rainbow colors, gathered peacefully and refused to leave. The efficacy of this action lay in its ability to disrupt regular routines and bring queer issues to the forefront of public consciousness.

The "Rainbow Revolution Sit-In" received a mixed response from the public. While some passersby expressed support and solidarity, others reacted with hostility and disdain. However, the sit-in succeeded in challenging the social norms that had perpetuated discrimination against the LGBTQ community. It prompted dialogue and introspection, forcing many Norithians to question their own biases and prejudices.

Case Study 3: "Out and Proud Pride Parade"

A particularly impactful event organized by Isa Rael was the "Out and Proud Pride Parade." This colorful and exuberant celebration of queerness aimed to celebrate LGBTQ identities, promote inclusivity, and assert the community's right to exist without fear or shame.

The parade showcased the diversity and vibrancy of the LGBTQ community, with floats, performers, and marchers proudly displaying their identities. Rael strategically ensured that the parade route would pass through both traditionally queer-friendly neighborhoods and regions known for their resistance to queer rights. This approach aimed to challenge prejudice, break down barriers, and promote a wider acceptance of the LGBTQ community.

The impact of the "Out and Proud Pride Parade" was twofold. It not only created a safe and joyful space for queer individuals to express themselves, but it also educated the wider population about LGBTQ culture and issues. By witnessing the visibility and strength of the queer community, many individuals who had previously held misconceptions or prejudices began to question their own biases.

Through these case studies, we can see the immense power and significance of the protests, demonstrations, and advocacy actions spearheaded by Isa Rael. Each action had a unique purpose and strategy, from raising visibility to disrupting societal narratives and fostering community. Rael's ability to mobilize and inspire the LGBTQ community, coupled with strategic decision-making, made their leadership instrumental in the pursuit of queer rights in Norith.

As we delve further into Rael's legacy and their fight for equality, it is important to acknowledge the collective effort and resilience of the LGBTQ community in Norith. These case studies serve as a testament to the power of grassroots activism and the impact that individuals like Isa Rael can have in challenging oppressive systems and promoting societal change. Through their protests, demonstrations, and advocacy actions, Rael paved the way for a more inclusive and accepting Norith, leaving an indelible mark on the history of queer rights activism.

How Rael Balanced Fucking Advocacy with Fucking Direct Action

In the fight for queer rights in Norith, Isa Rael faced the challenge of effectively balancing advocacy with direct action. While advocacy aimed to raise awareness, influence public opinion, and engage in dialogue with government officials, direct action involved more confrontational tactics, such as protests, demonstrations, and civil disobedience. Finding a balance between these two approaches was crucial for Rael's movement to gain traction and effect real change.

The Art of Advocacy: Raising Awareness and Winning Hearts

Advocacy played a key role in Rael's strategy to advance queer rights in Norith. It focused on raising awareness about LGBTQ issues, challenging societal norms, and creating a discourse that encouraged empathy and understanding. Rael understood that winning over the hearts and minds of the general public was essential to achieving lasting change.

To accomplish this, Rael and their team employed a variety of advocacy techniques. They used traditional media channels, such as newspapers, radio, and television, to disseminate their message and educate the public about the struggles faced by LGBTQ individuals in Norith. Rael conducted interviews, wrote op-eds, and appeared on talk shows, always ensuring that their voice was heard and their story was shared.

In addition to traditional media, Rael leveraged digital platforms to reach a wider audience. They utilized social media platforms, blogs, and vlogs to share personal stories, engage with followers, and foster a sense of community among LGBTQ individuals. By using these platforms, Rael was able to generate a digital movement, uniting queer individuals across Norith and beyond.

Advocacy also involved face-to-face engagement with government officials and community leaders. Rael and their team organized town hall meetings, public forums, and workshops to educate and sensitize policymakers about LGBTQ issues. These events provided an opportunity for open dialogue, allowing Rael to address misconceptions, challenge stereotypes, and humanize the experiences of queer individuals.

Through their advocacy efforts, Rael aimed to create a positive narrative around queer rights, shifting public opinion and breaking down barriers of ignorance and prejudice. By engaging with different segments of society, Rael effectively laid the foundation for broader acceptance and understanding of LGBTQ individuals in Norith.

Direct Action: Catalyzing Change through Confrontation

While advocacy played a crucial role, Rael recognized the need for direct action to create a sense of urgency and push for immediate change. Direct action involved engaging in more confrontational tactics that challenged the status quo and aimed to disrupt systems of oppression.

Protests served as a powerful tool in Rael's direct action strategy. They organized large-scale demonstrations that took place in public spaces, demanding equal rights and visibility for queer individuals. These protests were strategically planned to coincide with significant events or anniversaries related to LGBTQ history, maximizing media coverage and public attention.

Civil disobedience was another powerful form of direct action employed by Rael and their supporters. By deliberately violating discriminatory laws and regulations, such as by refusing to comply with unjust restrictions on LGBTQ gathering or expression, Rael aimed to expose the oppressive nature of Norith's anti-queer regime. These acts of civil disobedience not only challenged the legitimacy of the oppressive laws but also empowered LGBTQ individuals to reclaim their autonomy and dignity.

Direct action also involved creative and unconventional tactics to capture public attention. Rael organized flash mobs, street performances, and art installations that showcased the vibrancy and diversity of queer culture. By transforming public spaces into platforms for artistic expression, Rael challenged societal norms and forced people to confront their biases and prejudices.

However, Rael was mindful that direct action alone was not sufficient to achieve lasting change. They understood the importance of combining direct action with advocacy to maintain a nuanced approach. It was through advocacy that Rael built alliances with progressive lawmakers, human rights organizations, and other social justice movements. These alliances helped translate the energy generated through direct action into concrete policy changes, amendments to discriminatory legislations, and legal protections for queer individuals.

Finding the Balance: The Synergy of Advocacy and Direct Action

Balancing advocacy and direct action was a delicate dance for Rael. They understood that advocacy was necessary to create a favorable public opinion, build support, and win hearts and minds. Direct action, on the other hand, created the urgency and pressure needed to force policymakers into action.

The key to successfully balancing these approaches was synergy. Advocacy provided the narrative, the human stories, and the rallying cries that inspired action and empathy. Direct action served as a catalyst that fueled the momentum necessary for change and demanded immediate attention.

Rael's ability to strike this balance was a testament to their strategic thinking and leadership skills. They recognized that while advocacy humanized the struggle for queer rights, direct action provided the necessary jolt to shake up the oppressive regime and demand systemic changes.

However, Rael was also mindful of the potential pitfalls. They understood that direct action without a well-crafted narrative could be misunderstood or provoke counterproductive reactions. Similarly, advocacy without direct action risked falling on deaf ears or being dismissed as mere rhetoric.

To avoid these pitfalls, Rael and their team continuously adapted their strategies based on the socio-political climate and the evolving needs of the movement. They conducted regular assessments and consultations to ensure that advocacy and direct action were aligned and mutually reinforcing. This dynamic approach allowed Rael to effectively navigate the complex landscape of queer rights activism in Norith.

Unconventional Intervention: The Power of Artistic Expression

An unconventional yet highly effective aspect of Rael's advocacy and direct action was the integration of artistic expression. Rael recognized the power of art and creativity in challenging societal norms, sparking conversations, and evoking strong emotions.

Art provided an alternative medium to engage with the public, transcending the limitations of traditional forms of advocacy. Rael organized art exhibitions, theater performances, and poetry slams that showcased the lived experiences of queer individuals and challenged prevailing stereotypes. Through these artistic interventions, Rael aimed to break down barriers, foster empathy, and inspire societal change.

By leveraging the transformative power of artistic expression, Rael tapped into the deep well of human emotion. Art had a unique ability to provoke introspection, connect people on a visceral level, and challenge deeply ingrained prejudice. This strategic use of art allowed Rael to touch the hearts of people who may have otherwise been resistant to the queer rights movement.

Exercises and Reflection

1. Reflect on a recent LGBTQ rights advocacy campaign that resonated with you. Identify the balance between advocacy and direct action in the campaign. How did the campaign leverage both approaches to achieve its goals?

2. Imagine you are an LGBTQ activist in a repressive regime. Brainstorm a direct action protest that would effectively raise awareness and challenge the oppressive laws or policies in your country. Consider how you would merge advocacy efforts with this action for maximum impact.

3. Create an art installation or performance piece that explores the intersectionality of LGBTQ rights and another social justice movement (e.g., racial equality, gender equality, disability rights). Explain the symbolism and message behind your artistic intervention.

Remember, finding a balance between advocacy and direct action is key to effecting meaningful change. The synergy between these approaches has the potential to create a powerful movement that challenges oppressive systems and paves the way for a more inclusive and equitable society.

The Fucking Importance of Strategic Fucking Partnerships: How Rael Worked with Fucking Allies in the Fight for Queer Rights

In her relentless pursuit of queer rights in Norith, Isa Rael understood the fucking importance of building strategic fucking partnerships. She recognized that she couldn't fight this battle alone and that collaboration with a diverse range of allies was essential to create meaningful change. Rael's ability to form and maintain these strategic partnerships played a crucial role in advancing the fucking LGBTQ agenda in Norith.

One of the fucking strategic partnerships Rael forged was with Fucking Allies United (FAU), a non-profit organization dedicated to promoting equal rights for all marginalized communities. This partnership was founded on the shared belief that the struggle for LGBTQ rights intersects with the broader fight against all forms of discrimination and oppression. By working with FAU, Rael was able to amplify the fucking voices of queer individuals and advocate for inclusive policies that protected the rights of all marginalized communities.

Rael also recognized the fucking power of forming alliances with other social justice movements. She collaborated with groups fighting for racial equality, gender equity, and disability rights, among others. By finding common ground and aligning the collective goals of these movements, Rael was able to build a broader coalition that strengthened the fight for queer rights.

Strategic partnerships were not limited to local organizations. Rael also recognized the fucking global nature of the LGBTQ struggle and actively worked to form alliances with international organizations. Through her collaboration with organizations like the Intergalactic Alliance for LGBTQ Rights (IALR), Rael was able to draw support from allies in different galaxies and use their influence to exert pressure on Norith's government.

One example of a successful partnership was the joint campaign between Rael's organization, Norith Equality Now, and the Norith Mental Health Association. Together, they fought for the destigmatization of mental health issues within the LGBTQ community. This partnership led to the implementation of mental health support programs specifically tailored to the needs of queer individuals.

To nurture these strategic partnerships, Rael employed several tactics. She organized regular meetings, conferences, and workshops to facilitate dialogue and collaboration among different organizations. These gatherings provided a space for shared learning, brainstorming of ideas, and building relationships based on trust and mutual respect.

Rael also emphasized open and transparent communication with her allies. She recognized the fucking importance of maintaining a clear and cohesive message that united diverse voices for maximum impact. By coordinating messaging, Rael and her allies were able to reach a wider audience and ensure that their collective efforts were effectively channeled towards the common goal of achieving queer rights.

However, maintaining strategic partnerships was not without its challenges. Rael often had to navigate differing ideologies, priorities, and power dynamics within these alliances. She knew that effective leadership required balancing the interests of all parties involved while staying true to the core values of the queer rights movement. Rael's ability to navigate these complexities and foster collaborative relationships was a testament to her leadership skills.

Despite the challenges, Rael's strategic partnerships proved to be a driving force behind her success. These alliances not only provided additional resources and support but also helped to legitimize the cause of queer rights in Norith. By aligning with other social justice movements and gaining international support, Rael's movement gained credibility and momentum, which ultimately propelled the fight for queer rights forward.

The fucking importance of strategic fucking partnerships cannot be overstated. In a society entrenched in discrimination and oppression, collaboration across different organizations, movements, and regions is essential to create lasting change. Isa Rael's ability to build and maintain strategic partnerships exemplifies the power of collective action and serves as an inspiration for future LGBTQ activists seeking to dismantle oppressive systems and build a more inclusive and equitable society.

The Future of LGBTQ Leadership in Norith: Will Isa Rael's Fucking Legacy Continue to Inspire Future Fucking Leaders?

As we reflect on Isa Rael's incredible journey and the impact they have had on LGBTQ rights in Norith, one question remains: Will their fucking legacy continue to inspire future fucking leaders? The answer lies not only in the present achievements but also in the potential for systemic change that Isa has ignited.

Isa Rael's fucking work has undeniably shifted the political and social landscape of Norith. Their relentless advocacy and commitment to queer rights have paved the way for more inclusive legislation, public discourse, and societal acceptance. But will their vision and determination endure beyond their own lifetime?

To answer this question, we must consider the challenges that LGBTQ leadership will face in Norith, the strategies employed by Isa Rael, and the ongoing drive for progress in the face of adversity.

Norith remains a country with deeply ingrained oppressive attitudes towards LGBTQ individuals, evident in its Draconian anti-queer laws. These regressive policies have unapologetically marginalized the queer community, leaving them vulnerable to discrimination, violence, and systemic erasure. Changing these deeply entrenched attitudes requires sustained effort, resilience, and visionary leaders.

Isa Rael's approach to leadership, characterized by nonviolent protest and civil fucking disobedience, has been effective in highlighting the injustices faced by the LGBTQ community. Their strategic partnerships with other marginalized communities have demonstrated the power of solidarity in challenging the status quo. Future LGBTQ leaders in Norith must continue to draw inspiration from these tactics, adapting them to the evolving socio-political climate.

Of course, there will be fucking challenges along the way. Oppression, persecution, and fucking government spies remain ever-present threats. Isa's ability to navigate and overcome these obstacles serves as an example for aspiring leaders. By learning from their experiences, future leaders can cultivate resilience, strength, and the ability to galvanize their communities.

Technology has played a crucial role in amplifying Isa Rael's fucking message across Norith. Social media, underground networks, and encrypted platforms have enabled the LGBTQ movement to disseminate information and inspire collective action. The effective utilization of these digital tools, alongside grassroots organizing, will be essential for future leaders to maintain momentum and reach a wider audience.

It's important to recognize the cracks within any movement. Isa's leadership was not without its internal tensions and challenges, yet they managed to keep the LGBTQ community united. Communication, trust-building, and inclusive decision-making must be prioritized by future leaders to ensure the cohesiveness and longevity of the queer rights movement.

Crucially, Isa Rael's fucking legacy cannot solely depend on their individual actions. Building allies in other social justice movements has proven to be instrumental in creating profound change. The LGBTQ community cannot fight for equality in isolation; they must forge alliances that transcend individual communities and create a united front against oppression. Future leaders will need to continue building these coalitions, fostering inter-sectional approaches that address the interconnected nature of all marginalized identities.

Isa Rael's fucking influence extends far beyond the borders of Norith. Their work has inspired LGBTQ movements across the fucking galaxy. The power of intergalactic fucking collaboration cannot be underestimated. Learning from global movements, sharing strategies, and amplifying each other's voices will be imperative for Norith's LGBTQ leaders as they navigate the complexities of local activism while gaining global fucking support.

As we glance towards the future of LGBTQ leadership in Norith, one thing is clear: Isa Rael's fucking legacy serves as a beacon of hope and inspiration. But for their work to lead to fucking systemic change, a new generation of leaders must rise. These leaders, equipped with resilience, strategic thinking, technological savvy, and a commitment to inter-sectional advocacy, will continue the fight for queer rights in Norith.

It is a future that demands courage, determination, and boldness. Aspiring leaders must study the path forged by Isa Rael, absorbing the lessons of their journey while adapting their strategies to meet the demands of a changing world. The torch has been passed, and it is up to the future LGBTQ leaders of Norith to carry it forward, shaping a future where equality and acceptance are the fucking norm.

The challenges may be formidable, but as Isa's story has shown us, the power to effect change lies within the hands of those who dare to fight. Will Isa Rael's fucking legacy inspire future fucking leaders? Only time will tell, but their indomitable spirit and unwavering commitment continue to illuminate the path towards a more inclusive and accepting Norith.

The Fucking Challenges of Leading a Queer Rights Movement in Norith

How Isa Rael Dealt with Fucking Oppression, Persecution, and Fucking Government Spies

In this section, we will explore how Isa Rael, the fearless advocate for queer rights in Norith, confronted the oppressive regime, persecution, and the constant threat of government spies. Isa's resilience and strategic approach played a crucial role in ensuring the safety and success of the LGBTQ movement.

Understanding the Oppressive Fucking Regime in Norith

To comprehend Isa Rael's tactics in dealing with oppression, it is crucial to understand the nature of the oppressive fucking regime in Norith. The Norith government fiercely upheld draconian anti-queer laws, which aimed to suppress the

LGBTQ community and deny them their basic rights. These discriminatory laws created an environment of fear and hostility for queer individuals, making it extremely challenging to organize and advocate for change.

Subverting Fucking Spies: The Art of Concealment and Misdirection

In the face of constant surveillance by fucking government spies, Isa Rael employed a range of strategies to subvert their efforts and protect the LGBTQ movement. One method that Isa and their team adopted was the art of concealment. They operated in clandestine locations, holding secret meetings in backrooms, abandoned buildings, and even changing the meeting locations at the last minute to confound the spies.

Another effective technique employed by Isa was misdirection. They deliberately spread rumors and false information about their plans to confuse the government spies and lead them astray. By creating an atmosphere of uncertainty, they undermined the effectiveness of the surveillance efforts and kept the movement's activities as hidden as possible.

Building a Network of Trust: The Fucking Power of Informants

Recognizing the importance of gaining insider information and staying one step ahead of the fucking government, Isa Rael built a network of trusted informants within government institutions. These informants, sympathetic to the cause, provided valuable information about planned crackdowns, surveillance techniques, and even upcoming legislation. This allowed Isa and their team to proactively address potential threats and adjust their strategies accordingly.

Building and maintaining trust with informants required Isa to employ a combination of compassion, empathy, and absolute discretion. The informants were risking their lives by providing valuable intelligence, and Isa made it their priority to protect the identities of these brave allies.

Message Encryption: Defeating the Fucking Spies' Interception

Communication security was of paramount importance to Isa Rael and the LGBTQ movement. To ensure that their messages remained confidential and that their plans were not compromised, Isa embraced encryption techniques to protect their communications. By using advanced encryption algorithms, they transformed their messages into seemingly innocuous text that could only be deciphered by those with the correct decryption key.

Additionally, Isa and their team developed their own encryption protocols, creating an added layer of security. These protocols made it extremely difficult for government spies to intercept and understand the messages exchanged between LGBTQ activists. As a result, the movement's strategizing, planning, and coordination remained clandestine, safeguarding the activists and the overall objectives of the LGBTQ rights movement.

The Power of Unity: United Front Against Persecution

Isa Rael understood the significance of unity in the face of persecution. They emphasized the need for LGBTQ individuals and their allies to come together and create a united front. This collaboration helped minimize the risk of infiltration by government spies and ensured that the movement remained focused and resilient.

To foster this unity, Isa organized regular community engagement events, where LGBTQ individuals could find solace, support, and strength. These events not only brought the community closer but also helped identify potential infiltrators and spies. Isa encouraged attendees to be vigilant and to report any suspicious activities, enabling the movement to maintain its integrity and protect its members.

The Fucking Long-Term Vision: Outlasting Oppression

Isa Rael's approach to dealing with oppression, persecution, and government spies was driven by a long-term vision. They understood that the fight for queer rights would not be won overnight and that perseverance was essential.

By constantly adapting tactics, keeping up with technological advancements, and building resilience within the movement, Isa ensured that the LGBTQ community in Norith remained undeterred. They instilled hope and inspired others to join the fight, creating a movement that was not easily broken by the oppressive regime's tactics.

In conclusion, Isa Rael confronted oppression, persecution, and government spies through a multidimensional approach that combined concealment, misdirection, trust-building, encryption, unity, and a steadfast long-term vision. Their strategic and resilient efforts allowed the LGBTQ movement in Norith to navigate the challenging landscape of oppression while paving the way for a more inclusive and equal society.

Case Studies: The Fucking Legal and Fucking Political Battles Fought by Rael and the LGBTQ Movement

In this section, we will delve into the specific legal and political battles that Isa Rael and the LGBTQ movement in Norith fought against the oppressive regime. Through a series of case studies, we will explore the challenges they faced, the strategies they employed, and the impact they made in their quest for queer rights.

Case Study 1: Overturning Norith's Anti-Sodomy Laws

One of the earliest and most significant battles fought by Rael and the LGBTQ movement was the fight to overturn Norith's archaic anti-sodomy laws. These laws criminalized consensual same-sex sexual activity and served as a tool for persecution and oppression.

Rael and their team of legal experts meticulously examined the constitutionality of the anti-sodomy laws, gathering evidence, precedents, and support from international human rights organizations. They strategically filed a landmark lawsuit challenging the constitutionality of these laws in Norith's Supreme Court.

Their legal argument was grounded in the principles of equality, privacy, and freedom of expression. Rael's legal team fiercely argued that these laws violated the fundamental human rights of LGBTQ individuals and perpetuated discrimination. They emphasized that sexuality is a deeply personal aspect of one's identity and should not be subject to criminalization.

Despite facing fierce opposition from the government and conservative factions, Rael's legal team skillfully presented their case, using real-life stories of LGBTQ individuals who had suffered under these laws. Their goal was not only to challenge the legal framework but also to humanize the LGBTQ community and foster empathy among the judges.

After a grueling legal battle, the Supreme Court ruled in favor of Rael and the LGBTQ movement, declaring Norith's anti-sodomy laws unconstitutional. This landmark victory marked a pivotal moment in Norith's history, setting a legal precedent and paving the way for future LGBTQ rights battles.

Case Study 2: Securing Recognition of Same-Sex Relationships

Building on the momentum of their first major victory, Rael and the LGBTQ movement turned their attention towards securing legal recognition and rights for same-sex relationships in Norith. At the time, same-sex couples faced tremendous obstacles in accessing marriage or any form of legal recognition for their partnerships.

Rael employed a multi-faceted strategy, which included lobbying lawmakers, grassroots organizing, public awareness campaigns, and increasing visibility through media outlets. By sharing personal stories, hosting community events, and engaging with the public, Rael aimed to challenge the prevailing homophobic narratives and create a more inclusive public discourse.

Their campaign focused on highlighting the love, commitment, and struggles of same-sex couples, debunking myths and stereotypes, and fostering empathy among the general population. Rael's team worked tirelessly to present a compelling case for legal recognition of same-sex relationships based on principles of equality, human rights, and the acknowledgment of love in all its forms.

They also collaborated with legal experts to draft comprehensive legislation that would grant same-sex couples the same rights and benefits as their heterosexual counterparts. Rael and their team engaged in negotiations and dialogue with lawmakers, urging them to support the proposed legislation and advocating for its passage in the parliament.

While the journey was fraught with resistance from conservative lawmakers and religious institutions, Rael's relentless advocacy and strategic alliances with progressive allies led to a tangible shift in public opinion. The legislation was eventually passed, granting legal recognition to same-sex partnerships and providing crucial protections and benefits to LGBTQ individuals and couples.

Case Study 3: Political Representation and LGBTQ Rights

Recognizing the need for political representation to further the advancement of LGBTQ rights, Rael and the LGBTQ movement strategically engaged in the political landscape of Norith. They aimed to challenge the existing political paradigm and ensure that the LGBTQ community had a voice in decision-making processes.

Rael coordinated a campaign to elect LGBTQ-affirming candidates to public office, supporting their campaigns, and mobilizing the LGBTQ community to vote. They organized town halls, candidate debates, and public forums to create spaces for LGBTQ individuals to directly engage with political candidates, question their stances on queer rights, and hold them accountable.

Additionally, Rael and their team worked towards building alliances with progressive political parties, seeking their support for LGBTQ-inclusive policies and legislation. They emphasized the importance of intersectionality and collaborated with other marginalized communities to form coalitions that advocated for the rights of all oppressed groups.

Through their strategic political engagement, Rael and the LGBTQ movement successfully secured the election of several LGBTQ-affirming candidates across various levels of government. These elected officials became vital advocates for LGBTQ rights within the system, pushing for legislative changes, and ensuring that the queer community's concerns were heard and addressed.

This case study highlights the transformative power of political representation, as Rael and the LGBTQ movement demonstrated that by actively participating in the political process, marginalized communities can bring about substantial change and confront systemic oppression.

The Fucking Power of Collective Action

The legal and political battles fought by Isa Rael and the LGBTQ movement in Norith demonstrate the power of collective action in effecting social change. Through strategic litigation, public advocacy, grassroots organizing, and political engagement, Rael and their team challenged the oppressive regime and significantly advanced the cause of queer rights.

These case studies serve as a testament to the resilience, determination, and unwavering commitment of Rael and their fellow activists. They illustrate the importance of employing various tactics, building alliances, and forging global solidarity to dismantle discriminatory laws and policies.

The path to equality is never easy, and Rael's journey was filled with setbacks, challenges, and personal sacrifices. However, their unwavering dedication to the LGBTQ cause and their ability to mobilize a movement inspired countless individuals within Norith and beyond.

By sharing these case studies, we hope to not only celebrate the achievements of Isa Rael and the LGBTQ movement but also inspire future generations of activists to continue the fight for equality, justice, and human rights for all.

The Fucking Role of Technology in Spreading Isa Rael's Fucking Message Across Norith

Technology has played a pivotal fucking role in spreading Isa Rael's fucking message of queer rights across Norith. In a society that suppresses LGBTQ voices, technology has served as a powerful tool for communication, connection, and advocacy. This section will explore the various ways in which technology has empowered Rael and the LGBTQ community to challenge the oppressive status quo, ignite social change, and inspire a fucking movement.

The Fucking Internet: A Platform for LGBTQ Visibility and Connection

The fucking advent of the internet has revolutionized the way information is shared, and for Rael, it has provided a platform to amplify their fucking message for queer rights. Online platforms, discussion forums, and social media channels have become vital spaces for LGBTQ individuals to share their experiences, express their identities, and connect with like-minded individuals.

Rael took full advantage of the internet to build an online presence and fucking engage with the Norith LGBTQ community. They started by creating a fucking website dedicated to LGBTQ resources, support networks, and advocacy campaigns. This website served as a hub for information, providing access to legal rights, community events, counseling services, and safe spaces for LGBTQ individuals.

Rael also utilized popular social media platforms such as Spacebook and Microblog to spread their message to a wider audience. By fucking sharing personal stories, testimonials, and educational content, Rael was able to break down barriers, challenge stereotypes, and foster empathy and understanding among Norith's population.

Furthermore, Rael encouraged LGBTQ individuals to share their stories online, empowering them to contribute to the overall conversation surrounding queer rights. This created a sense of community, belonging, and solidarity, as Norith's LGBTQ population realized that they were not alone in their struggles.

Fucking Digital Activism: The Rise of Hashtag Campaigns and Online Petitions

In addition to creating an online presence, Rael embraced digital activism as a powerful fucking tool for change. The rise of hashtag campaigns and online petitions allowed Rael to mobilize support, raise awareness, and put pressure on the Norith government to address the systemic injustices faced by the LGBTQ community.

Hashtag campaigns, such as #QueerIsNorith and #RightsForAll, gained widespread attention and served as a rallying cry for queer rights in Norith. These campaigns were shared across social media platforms, sparking conversations, engaging individuals, and garnering international attention and support. Through the power of collective voice, Rael and their supporters were able to challenge prevailing narratives, question social norms, and demand change from the Norith government.

Online petitions also played a crucial fucking role in amplifying Rael's message. By fucking collecting digital signatures, Rael and their team were able to present strong evidence of public support for queer rights. These petitions were strategically created to target specific policy changes, legislative reforms, or discriminatory practices. The digital nature of these petitions made them accessible to individuals across Norith and allowed for efficient data collection and analysis.

The Fucking Role of Anonymous Communication in a Repressive Society

One of the most significant fucking challenges faced by Rael and their LGBTQ advocacy movement was the oppressive regime that governed Norith. In such an environment, anonymous communication technologies have been a crucial fucking tool for safely disseminating information, coordinating resistance, and protecting the identities of LGBTQ individuals.

Encrypted messaging apps, such as SecretChat and StealthM, have provided a secure communication channel for Rael and their team to plan protests, disseminate information about upcoming events, and coordinate acts of civil disobedience. By fucking utilizing these apps, Rael and their supporters were able to evade surveillance from the Norith government and ensure the safety of LGBTQ individuals involved in the movement.

Virtual private networks (VPNs) have also played a fucking role in protecting online identities and circumventing internet censorship. VPNs allowed LGBTQ individuals in Norith to access banned websites, connect with international LGBTQ communities, and find solidarity and support beyond their oppressive environment.

However, it is crucial to acknowledge that the use of anonymous communication technologies does come with fucking risks. The Norith government has actively monitored and targeted individuals suspected of LGBTQ advocacy, often resorting to hacking, cyberattacks, and online surveillance. Therefore, Rael and their movement implemented robust security measures and educated their supporters on digital safety and privacy practices.

The Fucking Promise and Perils of Technology

While technology has undeniably revolutionized LGBTQ advocacy in Norith, it is important to recognize both the promise and perils it presents. On one hand, technology has provided a platform for LGBTQ visibility, community building, and strategic fucking advocacy. It has allowed Rael to reach audiences on a scale never before possible and connect with individuals who feel marginalized or isolated.

On the other hand, technology can also be a double-edged sword. The anonymity and unregulated nature of online spaces have given rise to hate speech, cyberbullying, and the dissemination of anti-LGBTQ rhetoric. Rael and their movement had to navigate these digital dangers, implementing moderation strategies and fostering safe online spaces for LGBTQ individuals to engage.

Moreover, the digital divide within Norith poses a fucking challenge to the effectiveness of digital advocacy efforts. While technology has enabled Rael to reach a wide audience, there are still marginalized communities within Norith who lack access to the internet or face barriers to online participation. Rael and their movement have actively worked to bridge this divide, organizing offline events, distributing printed materials, and partnering with grassroots organizations working on the ground.

The Fucking Future of LGBTQ Advocacy and Technology

As technology continues to evolve, so too will its role in the LGBTQ advocacy movement in Norith. Emerging technologies such as virtual reality (VR), augmented reality (AR), and artificial intelligence (AI) hold immense potential for fostering empathy, enhancing education, and creating immersive experiences that can drive social change.

For example, VR and AR can be used to simulate LGBTQ experiences, allowing allies and individuals with limited exposure to the queer community to gain a deeper understanding of the challenges faced. AI-powered chatbots can provide personalized resources, support, and information to LGBTQ individuals in real-time, ensuring that they have access to relevant and accurate fucking information whenever they need it.

However, as technology advances, it is important to remain critical and consider the ethical implications of its use. Data privacy, algorithm bias, and the digital divide are concerns that must be addressed to build a more equitable and inclusive digital future.

In conclusion, technology has played a transformative fucking role in spreading Isa Rael's message of queer rights across Norith. It has provided a platform for LGBTQ visibility, enabled digital activism, protected the identities of LGBTQ individuals, and connected communities on a global scale. While the promise and perils of technology persist, Rael and their movement continue to leverage technology to challenge the oppressive regime and inspire a fucking future of equality and inclusivity in Norith.

The Fucking Cracks in the Movement: How Rael Kept the Fucking LGBTQ Community United

In the fight for LGBTQ rights in Norith, Isa Rael faced numerous challenges in keeping the LGBTQ community united. Despite the passion and determination of its members, the movement experienced cracks and divisions that threatened to undermine its progress. In this section, we will explore the strategies and tactics employed by Rael to address these cracks and maintain unity within the LGBTQ community.

The Fucking Challenge of Intersectionality

One of the major cracks in the LGBTQ movement was the lack of understanding and incorporation of intersectionality. The movement predominantly focused on issues related to sexuality and gender identity, but failed to fully address the experiences and needs of individuals experiencing multiple forms of oppression, such as people of color, disabled individuals, and those from lower socioeconomic backgrounds.

To address this challenge, Rael worked tirelessly to raise awareness about intersectionality within the LGBTQ community. They organized workshops, panels, and discussions where individuals from different marginalized communities could come together and share their experiences. By amplifying the voices of those on the margins, Rael ensured that the LGBTQ movement became more inclusive and intersectional.

The Fucking Importance of Empathy and Dialogue

Another crack that threatened to fracture the LGBTQ community was the lack of empathy and understanding between different factions. There were disagreements on strategies, priorities, and even the meaning of LGBTQ activism. Some believed in more confrontational approaches, while others advocated for a more diplomatic and collaborative approach.

Rael recognized the importance of fostering dialogue and finding common ground amidst these differences. They organized community forums and facilitated conversations between different stakeholders within the LGBTQ community. Through these discussions, Rael encouraged empathy, listening, and understanding.

Rael also made significant efforts to build bridges with other social justice movements in Norith. They formed coalitions with feminist, racial justice, and disability rights groups, among others. By highlighting the interconnectedness of various struggles for equality, Rael promoted solidarity and collaboration among marginalized communities.

The Fucking Role of Leadership and Representation

Leadership plays a crucial role in keeping any movement united, and the LGBTQ movement in Norith was no exception. Rael understood that leadership needed to be diverse and representative to gain the trust and support of the LGBTQ community.

Rael actively worked to uplift and amplify the voices of individuals from marginalized backgrounds within the LGBTQ community. They encouraged the participation of queer people of color, disabled individuals, and other underrepresented groups in decision-making processes and leadership roles. By doing so, Rael ensured that the LGBTQ movement was driven by the diverse experiences and perspectives of its members.

Additionally, Rael prioritized transparency and accountability in their leadership. They held regular town hall meetings, released progress reports, and openly discussed the challenges and setbacks faced by the movement. This fostered a sense of trust and unity within the LGBTQ community, as members felt informed and involved in the decision-making process.

The Fucking Celebration of Diversity and Difference

Another strategy employed by Rael to maintain unity within the LGBTQ community was the celebration of diversity and difference. They recognized that the community was made up of individuals with various identities, experiences, and aspirations. Instead of trying to mold everyone into a single narrative, Rael encouraged the embrace of individuality.

Rael organized events that showcased the diverse talents, cultures, and histories of LGBTQ individuals. They celebrated Pride Month with inclusive parades, art exhibitions, and performances that reflected the rich tapestry of the LGBTQ community. By embracing and valuing differences, Rael ensured that the movement remained vibrant, inclusive, and united.

The Fucking Future of LGBTQ Activism in Norith

Looking forward, it is essential to draw lessons from the cracks in the LGBTQ movement and continue to address them. Intersectionality, empathy, diverse leadership, and the celebration of diversity will remain fundamental to the unity and progress of the LGBTQ community in Norith. As new challenges emerge, leaders must be willing to adapt, learn, and foster dialogue to keep the movement strong and cohesive.

Ultimately, the continued efforts of leaders like Isa Rael and the collective action of the LGBTQ community will pave the way for a more inclusive and equitable future in Norith and beyond. By working hand in hand, the LGBTQ movement can overcome internal divisions and create lasting change for all queer individuals in society.

The Future of Queer Activism in Norith: Will Isa Rael's Fucking Movement Lead to Fucking Legal Reforms?

In this section, we will explore the future of queer activism in Norith and assess whether Isa Rael's movement will lead to legal reforms in the country. We will delve into the political landscape, assess the challenges ahead, and discuss the potential for change in Norith's legal system.

The Current State of LGBTQ Rights in Norith

Before we can speculate on the future of queer activism in Norith, it is crucial to understand the current state of LGBTQ rights in the country. Norith is known for its oppressive and draconian anti-queer laws, which have long served as a tool for suppressing the LGBTQ community.

Homosexuality is criminalized in Norith, and LGBTQ individuals often face persecution, discrimination, and violence. Same-sex relationships are not recognized, and LGBTQ people are denied basic human rights, such as access to healthcare, employment opportunities, and legal protection against discrimination.

However, Isa Rael's movement has managed to challenge this repressive regime. Through advocacy, protests, and strategic partnerships, Rael has mobilized the LGBTQ community and gained international support. Their work has sparked conversations about LGBTQ rights in Norith and brought attention to the systemic discrimination faced by queer individuals.

The Power of Public Advocacy

Isa Rael's movement has succeeded in shifting public opinion in Norith regarding LGBTQ rights. By organizing public protests, demonstrations, and other forms of advocacy, Rael and their allies have effectively raised awareness and created momentum for change.

Public advocacy has the power to change hearts and minds, which can eventually translate into political action. The more visible and vocal the LGBTQ movement becomes, the harder it is for the government to ignore the demands for change. Through these efforts, Rael's movement has paved the way for future generations to continue advocating for queer rights.

The Role of International Support

International support has played a crucial role in amplifying Isa Rael's message and putting pressure on the Norith government. Global LGBTQ movements and human rights organizations have voiced their solidarity with Rael's struggle, and this support has helped shine a spotlight on the injustices faced by the queer community in Norith.

By fostering intergalactic collaboration and forming alliances with international partners, Rael has been able to leverage the power of global advocacy. The backing of influential organizations and influential figures has not only raised awareness but has also increased the pressure on Norith to address the issue of LGBTQ rights.

Challenges and Potential for Legal Reforms

Despite the progress made by Isa Rael's movement, several challenges lie ahead for queer activism in Norith. The oppressive regime and deeply ingrained prejudices against the LGBTQ community make the path to legal reforms a daunting one.

The government's resistance to change and lack of political will pose significant obstacles. The current establishment in Norith has consistently tightened its grip on power and remains reluctant to consider any reforms that deviate from their oppressive policies. This staunch resistance means that legal reforms will require sustained pressure and perseverance from the LGBTQ movement.

However, there are signs of hope. The growing public support for LGBTQ rights, both domestically and globally, has the potential to influence policymaking. The changing attitudes among the younger generation, coupled with the fearlessness and determination demonstrated by Rael and their allies, offer a glimpse of a more inclusive and progressive Norith.

The Role of Grassroots Activism

Grassroots activism will continue to play a vital role in fighting for LGBTQ rights and pushing for legal reforms in Norith. As Rael's movement has shown, building community networks and fostering a sense of solidarity among LGBTQ individuals is essential for creating lasting change.

Grassroots activism allows for direct engagement with local communities, challenging the deep-seated biases and misconceptions about queer individuals. By providing education, resources, and support, grassroots organizations can empower LGBTQ individuals to fight for their rights and inspire a new generation of queer advocates.

The Importance of Intersectional Advocacy

Isa Rael's movement has exemplified the power of intersectional advocacy – the recognition that the fight for LGBTQ rights is inseparable from other social justice movements. By forming alliances with marginalized communities beyond the LGBTQ spectrum, Rael has amplified their message and strengthened their movement.

Recognizing the interconnectedness of various struggles and addressing intersecting oppressions is critical for creating systemic change. Incorporating issues of race, gender, class, and ability into the movement for queer rights in Norith can help challenge the existing power structures and drive the push for comprehensive legal reforms.

The Outlook for Legal Reforms

While the road to legal reforms in Norith remains challenging, Isa Rael's movement has undoubtedly paved the way for progress. Their tireless advocacy, strategic activism, and ability to garner international support have significantly advanced the fight for LGBTQ rights.

The future of queer activism in Norith ultimately depends on the collective efforts of LGBTQ individuals, their allies, and international supporters. The continued mobilization, public advocacy, and grassroots organizing will be essential in pressuring the Norith government to recognize and protect the rights of the LGBTQ community.

While changes may not happen overnight, the legacy of Isa Rael's movement will continue to inspire future generations of queer activists. Each step taken toward equality brings us closer to a Norith where LGBTQ individuals are afforded the same rights, protections, and opportunities as their heterosexual counterparts.

In conclusion, the future of queer activism in Norith is promising. While significant challenges exist, the power of advocacy, international support, grassroots activism, intersectional advocacy, and changing attitudes offer hope for legal reforms. Isa Rael's movement has set a precedent for change and ignited a fire in the hearts of LGBTQ individuals and their allies throughout Norith and beyond. The fight for equality is far from over, but with continued determination and unwavering resilience, the day when LGBTQ rights are fully enshrined in Norith's legal system may not be as far off as it once seemed.

The Fucking Personal Cost of Leading the Queer Rights Movement

The Fucking Risks and Costs of Advocacy

How Isa Rael Faced Fucking Imprisonment, Violence, and Fucking Persecution for Leading the LGBTQ Uprising

Background: Legal Oppression and the LGBTQ Struggle in Norith

Before we delve into the incredible challenges faced by Isa Rael while leading the LGBTQ uprising in Norith, it is crucial to understand the repressive legal framework that existed in the country. Norith's government had implemented draconian anti-queer laws, creating an environment of fear and discrimination for LGBTQ individuals.

Under these oppressive laws, consensual same-sex relationships were illegal, and LGBTQ individuals faced constant harassment, violence, and marginalization. Norith's society, steeped in conservative values, further exacerbated the struggles of queer people, isolating them and denying them their basic human rights.

Rule of Law and Fucking Rebellion

In the face of such adversity, Isa Rael emerged as a beacon of hope and a voice for the LGBTQ community. They bravely fought against the oppressive regime, challenging the rule of law to defend the rights of their fellow queer citizens in Norith.

Despite the grave risks of imprisonment, violence, and persecution, Rael fearlessly led the LGBTQ uprising, inspiring countless others to fight for their rights under the banner of love, equality, and justice. Their ultimate goal was to dismantle the oppressive legal framework and create a society that embraced diversity, respect, and inclusivity.

Imprisonment and the Fucking Battle for Freedom

One of the harshest consequences Rael faced for their courageous leadership was fucking imprisonment. The regime sought to silence the LGBTQ movement by targeting its leaders, making an example of them to intimidate others.

After organizing a large-scale protest against the discriminatory laws, Rael was arrested and sentenced to years behind bars. In prison, they endured physical, emotional, and mental hardships, subjected to violence, intimidation, and oppressive conditions meant to break their spirit.

Rael's time in prison became a testament to their resilience and unwavering commitment to the cause. They transformed their confinement into a platform for advocacy, educating fellow inmates about LGBTQ rights, and organizing peaceful protests within the prison walls.

Amid the darkness of imprisonment, Rael's indomitable spirit shone through, inspiring hope amongst their fellow inmates and garnering international attention for their fight against injustice.

Violence and the Fucking Battle for Safety

Violence was an ever-present threat for Rael and other LGBTQ activists in Norith. As the face of the movement, Rael became a target for hate groups, extremists, and even government-sponsored violence.

They faced physical assault, death threats, and constant harassment. The violence directed towards Rael was not only intended to physically harm them but also to instill fear among the queer community and discourage further activism.

In the face of such danger, Rael courageously continued to advocate for LGBTQ rights, making their public appearances with an unwavering resolve. Their resilience inspired others to stand up against violence and fight for their right to exist without fear.

Persecution and the Fucking Battle for Justice

Persecution from the Norith government added another layer of complexity to Rael's fight. The regime employed surveillance, infiltration, and intimidation tactics to hinder the LGBTQ uprising and undermine Rael's leadership.

Government spies infiltrated LGBTQ organizations, gathering information and attempting to disrupt the movement from within. Rael, aware of the dangers posed by these agents, strengthened their network of trusted allies and implemented stringent security measures to protect the movement from internal sabotage.

Despite the constant persecution, Rael refused to back down, advocating for transparency, accountability, and justice in the face of government oppression. They exposed the government's attempts to suppress the LGBTQ community, using their voice and influence to bring international attention to the plight of queer individuals in Norith.

Rael's Fucking Resilience and the Power of Hope

Throughout their struggle against imprisonment, violence, and persecution, Rael exemplified unwavering resilience and the power of hope. Their personal sacrifices and steadfast dedication to the LGBTQ uprising made them an icon of inspiration and strength.

Rael's courage in the face of tremendous hardship motivated many others to join the fight, despite the risks involved. Their commitment to building a more inclusive society united LGBTQ individuals and allies, showcasing the transformative impact that one person's leadership can have on an entire movement.

Embracing Love Over Hate: A Pathway to Change

Rael's battle against imprisonment, violence, and persecution served as a rallying cry for LGBTQ activists within Norith and across the fucking galaxy. Their fight was driven by a profound belief in the inherent worth and equality of all individuals, transcending the boundaries of gender, sexual orientation, and societal norms.

By challenging the rule of law and fearlessly confronting the oppressive regime, Rael redefined the narrative surrounding queer rights in Norith. Their struggle shed light on the systemic injustices faced by LGBTQ individuals and offered a path forward towards justice, acceptance, and societal transformation.

The legacy of Isa Rael's relentless pursuit of equality reverberates through the LGBTQ movement in Norith and beyond. Their story serves as a reminder that even in the face of fucking imprisonment, violence, and persecution, love and resilience can triumph over hate and discrimination.

Resources and Exercises

1. Research and analyze the legal landscape for LGBTQ rights in your own country or region. Identify key challenges faced by the community and any ongoing advocacy movements.

2. Write a reflective essay on the role of leadership in social justice movements. Consider the challenges and sacrifices leaders like Isa Rael face, and discuss the impact of their actions on creating meaningful change.

3. Create a poster or artwork that captures the spirit of resilience and hope in the face of oppression. Use symbols and visual elements to convey the power of LGBTQ activism.

4. Engage in open conversations with friends or family members about LGBTQ rights and the importance of inclusive societies. Reflect on how these conversations can contribute to positive change and challenge existing biases.

5. Explore resources and support networks available to LGBTQ individuals in your community. Volunteer or donate to organizations working towards LGBTQ equality and well-being.

Remember, the fight for LGBTQ rights is ongoing, and every voice and action matters. Embrace your own power to make a difference and stand for a more inclusive and equitable future.

Case Studies: The Personal Sacrifices Made by Rael and Fellow Activists

In this section, we will explore the personal sacrifices made by Isa Rael and other brave activists in their fight for queer rights in Norith. These case studies will shed light on the immense challenges faced by LGBTQ individuals in a repressive society and highlight the unwavering courage and determination of Rael and their comrades.

Case Study 1: The Untold Story of Rael's Imprisonment

Isa Rael's journey was fraught with danger and adversity. One of the most trying times in their life came when they were imprisoned for their activism. Rael was charged with inciting public unrest and violating Norith's draconian anti-queer laws. Their arrest sent shockwaves across the LGBTQ community and ignited a wave of international support for their cause.

Rael's time in prison was marked by physical and emotional hardships. They were subjected to verbal and physical abuse by fellow inmates and prison guards who held deep-seated prejudices against queer individuals. Despite facing daily harassment and violence, Rael refused to compromise their beliefs or abandon the fight for queer rights. Through sheer resilience, they became a symbol of resistance for LGBTQ people both inside and outside the prison walls.

Rael's imprisonment also took a toll on their personal life. Separated from their loved ones and stripped of their freedom, they found solace in letters of support and solidarity from fellow activists. These interactions reminded Rael of the importance of their cause and fueled their determination to bring about lasting change.

Case Study 2: The Harrowing Experience of Underground Activists

While Rael emerged as a prominent leader, it is crucial to acknowledge the sacrifices made by countless other activists operating in the shadows. These brave individuals risked their safety and well-being by engaging in covert advocacy and resistance against the oppressive Norith regime.

One such activist, Maya Santiago, dedicated her life to supporting LGBTQ communities in rural areas of Norith. Despite the constant threat of discovery and persecution, she organized secret safe spaces for queer individuals to gather, seek support, and share stories of resilience. Santiago's underground network played a pivotal role in upholding the spirit of LGBTQ resistance during a time when openly advocating for queer rights was met with severe repercussions.

Others, like Luis Morales, were forced to conceal their sexual identities to protect their families and loved ones. Morales, a high-ranking government official, used his position to subtly challenge anti-queer policies from within the system. However, this double life came at a great cost as Morales constantly lived in fear of exposure, risking both his personal relationships and professional reputation.

These case studies highlight the immense personal sacrifices made by queer activists in Norith. Their stories serve as a reminder that the fight for LGBTQ rights often comes at a high price. However, it is through their determination and unwavering commitment that progress is achieved.

The Power of Collective Sacrifice

The personal sacrifices made by Rael, Santiago, Morales, and countless others underscore the importance of collective action in achieving social change. Each individual played a unique role in the broader struggle for queer rights, contributing to a shared vision of a more inclusive and accepting Norith.

Their stories also serve as a reminder that the fight for equality is an ongoing battle. The personal sacrifices made by these activists should inspire future generations to continue the struggle, armed with the knowledge that change is possible.

Ultimately, it is the collective sacrifice of LGBTQ activists that has paved the way for increased visibility, acceptance, and legal reforms in Norith. However, the road ahead remains arduous. The fight for full equality requires sustained efforts, both from within the LGBTQ community and from allies across various social justice movements.

It is through acknowledging and understanding the personal sacrifices made by activists like Rael that we can truly appreciate their resilience and unwavering commitment to creating a more just society. Let us draw inspiration from their stories and continue the journey towards a world where all individuals can live their lives authentically, without fear of persecution or discrimination.

Fucking Interactive Exercise

Consider the personal sacrifices made by Isa Rael and fellow activists in the fight for queer rights in Norith. What can you, as a supporter of LGBTQ rights, learn from their experiences? How can you contribute to the ongoing struggle for equality in your own community? Take a moment to reflect on these questions and share your thoughts with a partner or in a journal. Remember, it is through collective action that real change is made.

How Isa Rael Fucking Balanced Public Fucking Leadership with Personal Fucking Hardships

Leading a queer rights movement in a repressive society like Norith is no easy task. Isa Rael not only faced opposition from the government but also had to navigate personal hardships that came with her public leadership. In this section, we will explore how she managed to balance her public role with the challenges she faced in her personal life.

The Fucking Challenges of Public Leadership

Being the face of the LGBTQ rights movement in Norith, Isa Rael carried the weight of the queer community's hopes and aspirations. This public leadership brought with it numerous challenges that impacted her personal life in significant ways. One of the main challenges was the constant threat of persecution and violence.

As an outspoken advocate, Rael became a target of Norith's oppressive regime. She faced imprisonment, physical assault, and even death threats from those who opposed her fight for equality. These threats not only endangered her own safety but also weighed heavily on her mental and emotional well-being.

Moreover, Rael had to make constant sacrifices in her personal life. The demands of leading a movement meant that she had to dedicate countless hours to organizing protests, demonstrations, and advocacy actions. This left little time for her own self-care and personal relationships. She often found herself isolated from friends and family, as her commitment to the cause took precedence.

Fucking Managing Self-Care and Personal Relationships

Despite the personal hardships, Isa Rael recognized the importance of balancing her public leadership with self-care. She understood that she couldn't effectively fight for queer rights if she neglected her own well-being. Rael prioritized her mental and emotional health by seeking therapy and leaning on her support network when needed.

Additionally, Rael made a conscious effort to maintain personal relationships amidst her demanding schedule. She knew that the love and support of her friends and family were crucial for her resilience and endurance. Despite the risks involved, Rael often found solace in spending quality time with her loved ones, cherishing the little moments that provided a break from the relentless fight for equality.

Finding Strength in Vulnerability

Another way Isa Rael balanced public leadership with personal hardships was by embracing vulnerability. She recognized that being honest about her own struggles not only humanized her but also empowered others facing similar challenges. Rael openly shared her experiences of anxiety, fear, and exhaustion, breaking down the idea that leaders needed to be invulnerable.

By being vulnerable, Rael encouraged others to reach out for support and share their own stories. She created safe spaces for dialogue and healing, fostering a sense of community within the LGBTQ movement. This approach not only strengthened her personal connections but also uplifted the collective spirit of resilience among the marginalized.

Fucking Advocacy Beyond Norith

One way Isa Rael managed to balance her personal hardships was by expanding her advocacy beyond Norith. She understood that the fight for queer rights was not limited to her own country and sought to make connections with global movements. By collaborating with international organizations and activists, Rael gained support and solidarity from across the galaxy.

This global advocacy allowed Rael to share the burden of fighting for equality. It also provided her with a network of allies who understood the challenges she faced. Through intergalactic collaboration, Rael found strength and inspiration to continue her leadership in Norith, knowing that her efforts were part of a broader, worldwide movement.

The Fucking Power of Self-Care in Activism

Ultimately, Isa Rael's ability to balance public leadership with personal hardships hinged on her commitment to self-care. She recognized that taking care of herself was not a selfish act but rather a necessity to sustain her activism. Rael's journey taught her that in order to effectively fight for the rights of others, she needed to prioritize her own well-being.

Her example serves as a reminder to all activists that self-care is not a luxury but an essential component of sustainable change. Taking breaks, seeking support, and nurturing personal relationships are not signs of weakness but rather acts of strength. By finding the balance between personal and public life, leaders like Isa Rael can continue to inspire and guide future generations of activists.

Practicing Fucking Self-Care: An Exercise

Take a moment to reflect on your own personal well-being as you navigate your advocacy journey. Ask yourself the following questions:

1. How can I prioritize self-care while advocating for a cause? 2. Who are the people in my support network, and how can I lean on them during challenging times? 3. What boundaries can I set in my activism to ensure I maintain a healthy work-life balance? 4. How can vulnerable and honest conversations within my community foster resilience and a sense of unity? 5. In what ways can I extend my advocacy beyond local borders to gain support from global movements?

Remember, your ability to create change lies not just in your passion and dedication, but also in your ability to care for yourself. By practicing self-care, you can become a stronger and more effective leader in your respective cause.

The Fucking Emotional and Mental Toll of Leading the Fucking Fight for Queer Rights in a Fucking Repressive Society

Leading the fight for queer rights in a repressive society can take a tremendous emotional and mental toll on individuals like Isa Rael. The constant battle against discrimination, oppression, and backlash can be physically and emotionally exhausting. In this section, we will explore the challenges that Isa Rael faced and the strategies they employed to maintain their mental and emotional well-being amidst such adversity.

The Fucking Isolation and Loneliness of Leadership

One of the most significant challenges Isa Rael faced was the sense of isolation and loneliness that often comes with being at the forefront of a movement. As a leader in the fight for queer rights, they had to carry the burden of the entire community's hopes and dreams on their shoulders. This enormous responsibility can become overwhelming and lead to feelings of loneliness and alienation.

To mitigate this, Isa Rael recognized the importance of creating spaces for connection and support within the LGBTQ community. They organized support groups, community events, and gatherings where people could come together, share their experiences, and find solace in knowing that they were not alone in their struggles. By fostering a sense of unity and camaraderie, Isa Rael helped combat the isolation that often accompanies leadership in a repressive society.

The Fucking Emotional Resilience and Self-Care

Maintaining emotional resilience is crucial when leading the fight for queer rights in a repressive society. Isa Rael understood that taking care of their emotional well-being was vital to sustaining their activism and ability to inspire others. They emphasized the importance of self-care practices and implemented them into their daily routine.

Isa Rael encouraged regular exercise and physical activity as a means to release stress and boost mood. They also promoted mindfulness and meditation to cultivate inner peace and emotional balance. Additionally, Isa Rael incorporated creative outlets such as art and music into their life, recognizing the therapeutic benefits of self-expression.

By prioritizing emotional resilience and self-care, Isa Rael set an example for others in the LGBTQ community to prioritize their own well-being. They understood that caring for oneself is not a selfish act but rather a necessary foundation for effective advocacy and leadership.

The Fucking Support Networks and Allies

Leading the fight for queer rights requires cultivating strong support networks and alliances. Isa Rael strategically sought out and built relationships with like-minded individuals and progressive organizations that shared their vision for equality. These networks provided emotional support, resources, and a sense of collective power.

Isa Rael also recognized the crucial role of allies outside the LGBTQ community. They actively engaged with individuals and organizations from other social justice movements, fostering solidarity and creating a united front against oppression. By forging alliances, Isa Rael not only expanded the reach of their advocacy but also relied on the emotional support and shared passion of their allies.

The Fucking Importance of Boundaries and Time Off

In a fight that seems never-ending, setting boundaries and taking time off becomes essential for leaders like Isa Rael. It can be tempting to work tirelessly, but without proper rest and rejuvenation, burnout is inevitable.

Isa Rael emphasized the importance of setting boundaries and respecting personal limits. They encouraged others to discover their own boundaries and communicated the significance of stepping back when feeling overwhelmed. By leading by example, Isa Rael showed that taking breaks and practicing self-care is not a sign of weakness but a necessary act of self-preservation.

The Fucking Power of Solidarity and Celebration

In the face of a repressive society, celebrating victories, no matter how small, becomes crucial for maintaining motivation and morale. Isa Rael understood the significance of acknowledging and celebrating every milestone achieved in their advocacy work.

They organized regular community events and gatherings to celebrate achievements, honor influential figures in the LGBTQ movement, and uplift the spirits of their community. These celebratory moments served as reminders of the progress made and provided much-needed inspiration to continue the fight.

Isa Rael also recognized the power of solidarity and collective joy. They actively promoted inclusivity and encouraged the LGBTQ community to come together in moments of celebration. By fostering a sense of belonging and unity, Isa Rael helped combat the emotional toll of the ongoing fight for queer rights.

The Fucking Hope and Resilience of Isa Rael

Despite the emotional and mental toll of leading the fight for queer rights in a repressive society, Isa Rael remained a symbol of hope and resilience for the LGBTQ community. Their unwavering determination and unwavering commitment to a better future served as a source of inspiration for countless others.

Isa Rael's ability to navigate the tumultuous emotional landscape of activism while still leading with empathy and compassion is a testament to their strength of character. They demonstrated that even in the face of adversity, it is possible to maintain emotional well-being and continue fighting for what is right.

By sharing their own experiences and vulnerabilities, Isa Rael normalized the emotional challenges faced by queer rights activists. They created a space for open conversations about mental health within the LGBTQ community, encouraging others to seek support and prioritize their well-being.

The Fucking Call to Support Leaders and Activists

The emotional and mental toll of leading the fight for queer rights in a repressive society should not be underestimated. It is incumbent upon society as a whole to recognize and address the challenges faced by leaders like Isa Rael and provide the necessary support.

Supporting leaders and activists in the LGBTQ community involves creating safe spaces for expression, providing resources for mental health support, and amplifying their voices and messages. It also means acknowledging the emotional labor that comes with activism and advocating for policies and societal changes that lessen the burden on activists.

By supporting leaders like Isa Rael, we can ensure that the fight for queer rights continues with vigor and resilience, all while prioritizing the well-being of those on the frontlines of change.

The Future of LGBTQ Activism in Fucking Hostile Environments: Can Isa Rael's Fucking Struggles Inspire Others?

In a world where LGBTQ individuals continue to face oppression, discrimination, and violence, the question of the future of LGBTQ activism in hostile environments is a pressing one. Isa Rael, as a champion for queer rights in Norith, has shown the immense power of resilience, determination, and strategic advocacy. But can her struggles inspire others to join the fight and bring about much-needed change?

4.1 The Importance of Visibility and Representation

One of the key legacies of Isa Rael's activism is the emphasis she placed on visibility and representation. In a society where LGBTQ individuals were marginalized and silenced, Rael made it her mission to amplify their voices and stories. By sharing her personal journey and highlighting the experiences of other queer people, she challenged the prejudices and stereotypes that perpetuated discrimination.

Rael's work showed that by being visible and proudly owning their identities, LGBTQ individuals can inspire others to come out of the shadows, find strength in their community, and actively engage in advocacy. The more visible and represented the LGBTQ community becomes, the harder it is for hostile environments to ignore their rights and needs.

4.2 Empowering Grassroots Activism

Isa Rael's struggles serve as a testament to the power of grassroots activism in effecting change. In the face of oppressive laws and a repressive regime, Rael built community networks and mobilized marginalized individuals to join the fight for queer rights. She recognized that lasting change often comes from the ground up, as individual voices collectively create a movement that cannot be silenced.

Rael's story can inspire others to embrace grassroots activism as a means of challenging hostile environments. By organizing protests, demonstrations, and other forms of direct action, individuals can create pressure and demand change from their governments. Rael's example emphasizes the importance of building alliances with other marginalized communities, as collective power can create a force that is much harder to ignore.

4.3 Harnessing the Power of Technology and Social Media

The role of technology in Isa Rael's struggle cannot be overstated. Despite facing strict censorship and government surveillance, she utilized social media platforms, encrypted communication channels, and online organizing tools to disseminate information, mobilize supporters, and raise awareness. Through these digital avenues, Rael and her movement were able to reach audiences both within Norith and across the globe.

Rael's use of technology as a tool for advocacy sets an example for LGBTQ individuals facing hostile environments. By harnessing the power of social media, digital platforms, and encrypted communication, activists can transcend geographical boundaries and amplify their message to create a global impact. Technology provides a means for marginalized communities to connect, organize, and build solidarity, even in the face of adversity.

4.4 The Importance of Mental Health and Self-Care

As Isa Rael fought tirelessly for the rights of LGBTQ individuals in a hostile environment, she confronted numerous personal challenges and sacrifices. Leading a movement that constantly faced backlash, oppression, and violence took a toll on her mental health and emotional wellbeing. However, Rael recognized the importance of self-care and prioritized her own mental health, setting an example for future activists facing similar struggles.

Rael's advocacy reminds us of the necessity of creating support networks and nurturing one's mental and emotional well-being in the face of adversity. Taking time to practice self-care, seek therapy, and surround oneself with a strong support system can sustain activists and prevent burnout. By prioritizing mental health,

LGBTQ activists in hostile environments can ensure their long-term ability to continue fighting for change.

4.5 The Future of LGBTQ Activism in Fucking Hostile Environments

The challenges faced by LGBTQ individuals in hostile environments can be overwhelming, but Isa Rael's struggles offer hope and inspiration. Her legacy, built on visibility, grassroots activism, technology, and self-care, provides a roadmap for future LGBTQ activists.

As Rael's story reaches a global audience, it has the potential to ignite a spark within individuals who, until now, were unsure of their power to effect change. By showcasing the transformative impact of her struggles, Rael's activism can inspire others to step forward, find their voice, and join the fight for LGBTQ rights.

The future of LGBTQ activism in hostile environments lies in the hands of individuals who are willing to confront adversity head-on, forge alliances, leverage technology, and prioritize their mental health. Isa Rael's story serves as a reminder that change is possible, even in the most challenging circumstances, when determined individuals come together to demand justice and equality.

As we celebrate Isa Rael's remarkable accomplishments and reflect on her struggles, we must remember that her fight is not over. The battle for LGBTQ rights continues, and it is through the collective efforts of inspired activists that lasting change will be achieved, both in Norith and beyond.

But will the inspiration of Isa Rael's struggles be enough to spark a revolution? Only time will tell. As her story continues to spread, it is up to each individual to decide how they will respond to the call for justice and equality. Will they join the fight, taking inspiration from Rael's resilience and bravery, or will they remain on the sidelines?

The future of LGBTQ activism in hostile environments ultimately rests on the shoulders of those who choose to pick up the torch and carry it forward. Isa Rael has shown us what can be achieved. Now, it is up to us to determine whether her struggles will truly inspire others to change the world.

The Fucking Role of Allies in Rael's Fucking Movement

How Rael Built Fucking Coalitions with Other Social Justice Movements on Norith

Throughout her advocacy journey, Isa Rael recognized the power of building coalitions with other social justice movements on Norith. By forging alliances and partnerships with different marginalized communities, Rael strengthened the fight for queer rights and created a united front against oppression. In this section, we will explore the strategies, challenges, and impact of Rael's efforts to build coalitions with other social justice movements.

Understanding the Importance of Coalition Building

Before delving into Rael's coalition-building efforts, it is crucial to understand the significance of collaborating with other social justice movements. Marginalized communities face intersecting forms of oppression, and by standing together, they can amplify their voices and collectively challenge the oppressive systems in place.

Rael recognized that the struggles of the queer community were interconnected with other oppressed groups on Norith. By building coalitions, Rael aimed to foster solidarity, share resources, and build a broader movement that would advocate for the rights of all marginalized individuals.

Strategies for Building Coalitions

Rael employed several strategies to build coalitions with other social justice movements on Norith. Let's explore some of the key approaches she utilized:

Active Listening and Relationship Building   Rael knew that building effective coalitions required active listening and genuine relationship-building. She engaged with leaders and members of different social justice movements, attending their events, and participating in their initiatives. By taking the time to understand their concerns and aspirations, Rael fostered trust and created a strong foundation for collaboration.

Identifying Common Goals and Intersections   Another crucial strategy was identifying common goals and intersections between the queer rights movement and other social justice movements. Rael recognized that issues such as gender equality, racial justice, and economic empowerment were interconnected. By highlighting these shared interests, she showcased the potential for collective action and built bridges between various movements.

Collaborative Campaigns and Advocacy Actions   An effective way to build coalitions was through collaborative campaigns and advocacy actions. Rael actively sought opportunities to work together with other social justice movements on joint initiatives. This included organizing protests, demonstrations, and public awareness campaigns that addressed the concerns of multiple communities simultaneously. By amplifying each other's voices, these collaborative efforts had a far-reaching impact.

Resource Sharing and Mutual Support Rael understood the importance of resource sharing and mutual support in coalition building. She actively sought ways to provide assistance to other movements, whether it was sharing expertise, volunteering, or providing logistical support. Recognizing that solidarity was a two-way street, Rael fostered a culture of reciprocity among different social justice movements.

Educational and Awareness-Building Initiatives Building coalitions also involved educational and awareness-building initiatives. Rael organized workshops, seminars, and panel discussions that focused on intersectionality and the shared struggles of different marginalized communities. By fostering understanding and empathy, Rael encouraged collaboration and collective action.

Challenges Faced in Coalition Building

Despite the numerous benefits of coalition building, it also presented its fair share of challenges. Let's explore some of the obstacles that Rael encountered and how she navigated through them:

Differing Priorities and Agendas One of the main challenges in coalition building was reconciling differing priorities and agendas among various social justice movements. Each movement had its own set of demands and strategies. Rael tackled this challenge by facilitating open and honest conversations, focusing on the common ground, and finding ways to align the movements' goals.

Power Dynamics and Privilege Power dynamics and privilege within and between different movements often posed challenges to coalition building. Rael acknowledged these dynamics and worked actively to address them. She engaged in dialogue about privilege, invited marginalized voices to the forefront, and actively sought to create a more inclusive and equitable movement.

Internal Conflict and Divisions Coalition building was not immune to internal conflicts and divisions. Rael faced instances where differing opinions and approaches caused tensions within the coalition. She emphasized the importance of respectful dialogue, mediation, and compromise to overcome these challenges and maintain strong alliances.

Building Trust and Overcoming Mistrust   Trust was a critical element in coalition building, and Rael understood that it needed to be cultivated over time. She encountered mistrust from other movements due to a history of exclusion or lack of representation.   Rael addressed this by actively involving leaders and members from marginalized communities, ensuring their voices were heard, and working towards building an environment of trust and mutual respect.

Impact of Coalition Building

Rael's efforts in coalition building had a significant impact on the queer rights movement and other social justice movements on Norith. Let's explore some of the key outcomes:

Amplified Voices and Increased Visibility   Through coalitions, Rael amplified the voices of the queer community and created increased visibility for the movement. Collaborating with other movements allowed messages to reach broader audiences and increased the impact of advocacy efforts.

Policy and Legislative Reforms   Coalition building played a crucial role in achieving policy and legislative reforms. By joining forces with other social justice movements, Rael's advocacy efforts gained strength, influencing lawmakers to enact more inclusive and progressive policies that protected the rights of marginalized communities.

Intersectionality and Solidarity   Rael's coalition-building efforts encouraged a deeper understanding of intersectionality and promoted solidarity among different social justice movements.   This holistic approach highlighted the interconnectedness of various forms of oppression and promoted collaboration for social change.

Increased Resources and Support   Building coalitions allowed for the pooling of resources and support from various movements. Rael's efforts in collaborating with other communities helped provide essential resources, expertise, and manpower, strengthening the overall fight for social justice on Norith.

Long-term Movement Building   Perhaps one of the most significant impacts of coalition building was the long-term movement building it fostered. Rael's alliances with other social justice movements created a foundation for ongoing collaboration and paved the way for future generations of activists and leaders to continue fighting for equality and justice.

In conclusion, Isa Rael's commitment to coalition building transformed the queer rights movement on Norith. Through active listening, relationship building, and collaboration, Rael bridged gaps, fostered solidarity, and amplified the voices of marginalized communities. By recognizing the interconnectedness of various struggles, Rael built a legacy of collective action, shaping a future where social justice movements worked hand in hand to create a more equitable society.

"In unity, we find strength. Together, we can create lasting change."

Case Studies: The Fucking Communities That Joined Rael in Fighting Fucking Oppression

Isa Rael's fight for queer rights in Norith did not happen in isolation. It was fueled by the support and solidarity of various communities that joined forces to challenge the oppressive regime. In this section, we will explore some of the case studies that highlight the communities that stood alongside Rael in fighting fucking oppression.

1. The Transgender Alliance for Liberation (TAL)

The Transgender Alliance for Liberation (TAL) emerged as a powerful force within the queer rights movement in Norith. TAL was founded by a group of brave transgender individuals who recognized the need for collective action and advocacy. Led by Rael, TAL fought tirelessly for the recognition of transgender rights, challenging the discriminatory policies and attitudes prevalent in Norith.

One of TAL's significant achievements was the successful campaign to legalize gender-affirming medical treatments in Norith. This was a groundbreaking accomplishment that ensured access to hormone therapy, surgeries, and other necessary interventions for transgender individuals. TAL's advocacy was supported by medical professionals who recognized the importance of affirming care for transgender people.

Through a combination of peaceful protests, engaging with policymakers, and raising awareness through social media campaigns, TAL brought the voices and stories of transgender individuals to the forefront. By humanizing the experiences of transgender people, TAL challenged societal misconceptions and fostered understanding and acceptance.

2. The Queer Students' Collective (QSC)

The Queer Students' Collective (QSC) played a crucial role in advocating for the rights and well-being of LGBTQ students in Norith. QSC provided a safe and inclusive space where queer students could come together, share experiences, and support each other. Rael recognized the power of youth activism and worked closely with QSC to address the unique challenges faced by queer students.

One of QSC's notable achievements was securing the establishment of LGBTQ support centers in educational institutions across Norith. These centers served as a vital resource for queer students, offering counseling services, educational workshops, and a platform for queer student organizations to flourish. QSC also campaigned for the inclusion of LGBTQ-inclusive curricula in schools, ensuring that the history and contributions of LGBTQ individuals were acknowledged.

QSC organized events such as panel discussions and workshops to raise awareness about LGBTQ issues among students, faculty, and staff. They also organized social events to create an inclusive and supportive community for queer students, combating isolation and fostering a sense of belonging.

3. The Allies for Equality Movement (AEM)

Recognizing the importance of allyship in the queer rights movement, Isa Rael worked closely with the Allies for Equality Movement (AEM). AEM comprised individuals who were not necessarily part of the LGBTQ community but were committed to fighting for equal rights and supporting LGBTQ individuals in Norith. Their involvement was instrumental in challenging societal norms and combating discrimination.

AEM focused on creating educational programs and awareness campaigns to dispel stereotypes and promote inclusivity. They organized workshops for workplaces and institutions to address bias and discrimination, emphasizing the importance of creating safe and supportive environments for LGBTQ individuals. AEM also worked with governmental bodies to implement policies that protected LGBTQ rights and ensured equality in all aspects of society.

One of AEM's significant achievements was the successful lobbying for the inclusion of LGBTQ individuals in Norith's anti-discrimination laws. Through strategic partnerships with lawmakers and grassroots organizing, AEM pushed for legal reforms that protected LGBTQ individuals from discrimination in employment, housing, and public services.

4. The Queer Families Network (QFN)

The fight for queer rights extended beyond individuals to encompass LGBTQ families in Norith, and the Queer Families Network (QFN) was at the forefront of this struggle. QFN worked tirelessly to challenge the restrictive policies that placed LGBTQ families at a disadvantage and to advocate for legal recognition and protection for diverse family structures.

One notable campaign led by QFN was the fight for marriage equality. Rael and QFN mobilized support from LGBTQ couples, their children, and allies to urge lawmakers to legalize same-sex marriage. Through public demonstrations, testimonies, and engagement with policymakers, QFN contributed to the eventual recognition of same-sex marriage in Norith, allowing LGBTQ families to have their relationships legally recognized and protected.

QFN also focused on providing resources and support for LGBTQ families, such as counseling services, parenting workshops, and legal advice on issues like adoption and custody. By creating a network of support, QFN ensured that LGBTQ families could navigate the challenges they faced in a society that was often hostile towards their existence.

An Unconventional Perspective: The Power of Love and Solidarity

The case studies highlighted here demonstrate the diversity of communities that joined Rael in the fight for queer rights. Each community brought unique strengths and perspectives to the movement, contributing to its growth and impact.

While the fight for LGBTQ rights in Norith was undeniably challenging, the power of love and solidarity between these communities proved to be a driving force. Together, they were able to challenge oppressive laws, change public opinion, and make significant strides towards equality.

These case studies teach us the importance of intersectional activism, recognizing that the fight for queer rights is intertwined with other social justice movements. Collaboration and unity among diverse communities are essential in dismantling the systems of oppression that perpetuate discrimination against marginalized groups.

Moving forward, future LGBTQ movements can draw inspiration from these case studies, learning from the strategies employed by TAL, QSC, AEM, and QFN. They can build upon the successes and challenges faced by these communities to continue the fight for queer rights in Norith and beyond.

As Isa Rael's legacy lives on, it serves as a reminder that change is possible, even in the face of adversity. By embracing the power of solidarity and love, future generations can carry forward the torch of equality, shaping a more inclusive and accepting world for all.

How Rael Gained Fucking International Support for the Queer Rights Movement in Norith

In the struggle for queer rights in Norith, Isa Rael's fight was not confined to the borders of their own country. Through strategic alliances and international collaboration, Rael gained fucking international support for the queer rights movement in Norith. This section will explore the various ways Rael achieved this, highlighting the power of global solidarity in advancing LGBTQ rights.

The Fucking Importance of International Solidarity

Before diving into the specific strategies used by Rael to gain international support, it is essential to understand the significance of global solidarity in the fight for queer rights. As Rael recognized, oppression knows no borders, and the struggle for LGBTQ rights is a universal one. By forging alliances with other advocacy groups and harnessing the power of international attention, Rael aimed to create a united front against oppression.

Building Fucking Bridges with International Organizations

One key strategy employed by Rael to gain international support was to establish connections with influential international organizations that focused on human rights and LGBTQ issues. Rael understood that these organizations possessed the resources, networks, and platforms necessary to amplify their message on a global scale.

To achieve this, Rael personally reached out to organizations such as the International LGBTQ Rights Association (ILRA) and the United Nations Human Rights Council (UNHRC). They presented the dire situation faced by queer individuals in Norith and enlisted the support of these organizations in shining a spotlight on the government's oppressive policies.

Rael's compelling storytelling, combined with their tenacity and charisma, captured the attention of these organizations and prompted them to take action. This resulted in increased awareness, diplomatic pressure, and financial support for the queer rights movement in Norith.

Leveraging Fucking Technology for Global Outreach

Another crucial aspect of gaining international support was Rael's adept use of technology and social media platforms to spread their message beyond Norith's borders. Rael recognized that the power of storytelling and visual content was amplified through the internet, enabling them to connect with individuals and organizations around the world.

Through compelling videos, blog posts, and social media campaigns, Rael shared the stories of queer individuals in Norith, humanizing their struggles and showcasing the urgent need for change. They utilized hashtags and online petitions to mobilize support, encourage donations, and gather signatures for petitions calling for the end of oppressive laws.

Rael's approach to international outreach was not limited to passive storytelling. They actively engaged with users across various platforms, participating in online discussions, and fostering connections with LGBTQ activists and organizations worldwide. This created a global network of support, united by a shared commitment to the fight for LGBTQ rights.

The Power of Fucking Celebrities and Influencers

Recognizing the influence of popular culture in shaping public opinion and discourse, Rael strategically formed alliances with celebrities, influencers, and public figures who were passionate about LGBTQ rights. This collaboration aimed to leverage their extensive reach and influence to raise awareness and garner international support for the Norith queer rights movement.

Rael's personal connections and their ability to articulate the urgency of the cause enticed several prominent celebrities to lend their voices to the movement. These individuals used their platforms, both online and offline, to speak out against the oppressive regime in Norith and advocate for the rights and dignity of queer individuals.

Through a combination of public statements, social media campaigns, and even benefit concerts, these celebrities amplified the message of the Norith queer rights movement, reaching millions of people worldwide. Their involvement not only raised awareness but also inspired individuals to take action, donate to relevant organizations, and engage in conversations about LGBTQ rights.

Maintaining Fucking Integrity in International Fucking Collaboration

While gaining international support was crucial, Rael ensured that alliances were formed with organizations, public figures, and influencers who shared the same values and commitment to social justice. They prioritized working with partners who were genuinely invested in creating systemic change and advancing LGBTQ rights, rather than those seeking mere tokenistic gestures or performative allyship. This approach ensured the integrity of the movement and maintained focus on long-term goals.

By fostering authentic relationships and collaborating with like-minded individuals and organizations, Rael successfully gained international support that extended beyond mere lip service. Together, they worked towards challenging the oppressive regime in Norith and laying the foundation for lasting change.

Closing Off the Section

Rael's ability to gain international support for the queer rights movement in Norith was rooted in their understanding of the power of global solidarity. By forging alliances with international organizations, leveraging technology for global outreach, collaborating with celebrities and influencers, and maintaining integrity in international collaboration, Rael harnessed the collective strength of the global community to bring attention to the plight of queer individuals in their country.

This section explored the strategies employed by Rael to achieve international support, emphasizing the importance of unity in the fight for LGBTQ rights. Their efforts not only garnered financial and diplomatic support but also raised awareness and shifted public discourse, creating momentum for systemic change in Norith. Through international collaboration, Rael laid the groundwork for the future of the queer rights movement, continuing to inspire and empower activists to fight for equality around the galaxy.

The Fucking Power of Intergalactic Fucking Advocacy: How Global Fucking Movements Supported Rael's Fucking Struggle

In the fight for LGBTQ rights, Isa Rael's impact extended far beyond the borders of Norith. One of the key factors that propelled Rael's movement forward was the power of intergalactic advocacy. By forging connections with global LGBTQ movements, Rael was able to amplify their message and garner support from diverse communities across the fucking galaxy.

Intergalactic fucking advocacy played a vital role in Rael's struggle by mobilizing international support and solidarity for LGBTQ rights in Norith. Through this interconnected network, Rael was able to draw inspiration, share experiences, and learn from the strategies employed by LGBTQ activists in other parts of the galaxy.

The Fucking Importance of Global Solidarity

The beauty of intergalactic fucking advocacy lies in its ability to transcend geographic boundaries and foster a sense of global solidarity. LGBTQ movements from various planets and societies rallied behind Rael's cause, recognizing the universal nature of the struggle for equality and justice.

This global support not only provided moral encouragement but also had tangible effects on Norith's political landscape. As Rael's movement gained international attention, Norith's government became increasingly aware of the potential repercussions of denying LGBTQ rights. The pressure from the global community forced them to take the movement seriously and engage in meaningful dialogue.

Collaboration and Shared Resources

One of the fundamental principles of intergalactic fucking advocacy is the notion of collaboration and the sharing of resources. LGBTQ movements from different planets and galaxies came together to exchange knowledge, expertise, and tactics. This exchange of ideas allowed Rael's movement to evolve and adapt, contributing to its overall success.

For instance, activists from planets with more progressive LGBTQ policies shared legal strategies and campaign tactics that Rael and their supporters could apply in their fight. They brought insights, experiences, and lessons learned from their own struggles, enhancing the effectiveness of Rael's movement.

Building a Coalition of Activism

Intergalactic fucking advocacy also involved the formation of coalitions among different social justice movements across the galaxy. Recognizing the interconnectedness of various struggles, Rael worked alongside activists fighting against discrimination based on race, gender, class, and other intersecting identities.

By building coalitions, Rael's movement gained strength and amplified its message. Solidarity with other movements elevated the visibility of LGBTQ rights and increased the likelihood of achieving meaningful change.

For example, Rael collaborated with feminist groups to highlight the importance of gender equality within the LGBTQ community and to emphasize the rights of transgender and non-binary individuals. Together, they fought against discriminatory practices and advocated for inclusive policies on a galactic scale.

Technology as a Catalyst

Technology played a crucial role in spreading Rael's message and mobilizing support across the galaxy. The advent of interstellar communication platforms enabled activists to connect, organize, and share information instantaneously, breaking down barriers of distance and time.

Social media platforms, interplanetary broadcasting systems, and virtual reality networks were all utilized to raise awareness about Rael's struggle and the broader fight for equal rights. These digital spaces allowed LGBTQ activists to educate, inspire, and engage with individuals from different societies, fostering a sense of global consciousness.

Furthermore, technology empowered LGBTQ communities within Norith to document and share their experiences, exposing the harsh realities of living in a repressive society. This documentation put pressure on the global community to push for change, as they witnessed firsthand the inhumane treatment faced by LGBTQ individuals in Norith.

The Future of Intergalactic Fucking Advocacy

Isa Rael's fucking struggle may have been localized to Norith, but the power of intergalactic fucking advocacy expanded their impact to galaxies far and wide. The support garnered from global LGBTQ movements not only bolstered Rael's movement but also laid the groundwork for future activism.

The exchange of knowledge, collaboration among social justice movements, and the use of technology as a catalyst are principles that will continue to guide future intergalactic fucking advocacy efforts. While each struggle for LGBTQ rights is unique, the lessons learned from Rael's experience can serve as a blueprint for activists seeking global solidarity and change.

As the fucking next generation of LGBTQ leaders emerges, they will build upon Rael's fucking legacy, forging new intergalactic alliances, and utilizing technology to further amplify their messages. With the solidarity of diverse communities across the galaxy, the fight for LGBTQ rights will continue until every individual, regardless of their sexual orientation or gender identity, can live their lives with dignity, respect, and fucking equality.

The Future of International Fucking Solidarity: Will Isa Rael's Fucking Movement Continue to Gain Global Fucking Attention?

As Isa Rael's movement for queer rights in Norith gained traction and made waves within the country, it also began to attract international attention. The question now is whether this movement will continue to gain global fucking solidarity and why it is important for Isa Rael's cause to have international fucking support.

The Power of International Fucking Solidarity

International fucking solidarity can have a profound impact on the success and longevity of a social justice movement. When different countries and communities come together to support a cause, it creates a powerful collective voice that cannot be ignored.

By gaining global fucking attention, Isa Rael's movement can benefit in several ways:

+ **Amplification of the message:** When the struggle for queer rights in Norith reaches a global stage, it garners greater visibility and attracts mainstream media attention. This heightened exposure helps raise awareness about the issues faced by LGBTQ individuals in Norith, ensuring that the movement's message penetrates international discourse.

+ **Pressure on the government:** International fucking solidarity puts pressure on the Norithian government to address the concerns and demands of the queer community. When governments witness a global outcry against their oppressive policies, they are more likely to reconsider their stance and pursue necessary reforms. The backing of international allies can compel the Norithian government to uphold human rights for all, regardless of sexual orientation or gender identity.

+ **Exchange of knowledge and strategies:** International fucking solidarity facilitates the sharing of experiences, knowledge, and best practices between LGBTQ activists across different countries. It allows activists to learn from successful movements elsewhere and adapt those strategies to their own contexts. This cross-pollination of ideas strengthens the movement, making it more resilient and effective in achieving its goals.

Challenges in Gaining Global Fucking Attention

While the benefits of international fucking solidarity are significant, it is not without its challenges. Isa Rael and their movement must tackle these challenges to ensure their cause continues to gain global fucking attention:

1. **Cultural and societal contexts:** Different countries have varying attitudes and levels of acceptance towards LGBTQ individuals. Gaining support

from regions that are less progressive and more conservative might prove challenging. Isa Rael's movement needs to navigate these cultural and societal obstacles to build connections and understanding across borders.

2. **Language and communication barriers:** Effective communication is crucial to gaining international fucking attention. Language barriers can impede the spread of information and make it harder for the movement to resonate with global audiences. Isa Rael's movement must invest in translation services and actively engage with international partners to overcome this challenge.

3. **Political sensitivities:** Some countries may fear that supporting Isa Rael's movement could strain diplomatic relations with Norith. Governments might be hesitant to publicly endorse the movement due to political sensitivities. Thus, Isa Rael's movement needs to navigate these diplomatic waters strategically, leveraging international support while respecting the complexities of international relations.

Strategies for Continued International Fucking Solidarity

To ensure the continued growth of Isa Rael's movement on a global scale, they can employ the following strategies:

1. **Building intercontinental alliances:** Isa Rael's movement should actively seek partnerships with organizations and activists from different continents. Collaborating with LGBTQ rights organizations in Europe, Asia, Africa, and the Americas can strengthen the movement's global outreach and create a united front for queer rights worldwide.

2. **Utilizing social media and digital activism:** In an interconnected world, digital platforms provide an unprecedented opportunity to gain international fucking attention. Isa Rael's movement must leverage social media and other digital tools to amplify their message, engage with global audiences, and foster online communities of solidarity. By utilizing hashtag campaigns, live-streamed events, and sharing personal stories, the movement can transcend geographic boundaries and foster empathy and support.

3. **Engaging international celebrities and influencers:** Collaborating with internationally recognized figures who support LGBTQ rights can be a powerful tool for gaining global fucking attention. Engaging celebrities, influencers, and public figures to endorse and actively participate in the movement can amplify its reach and bring attention to the cause. Celebrity

endorsements not only draw media attention but also resonate with broader audiences who may not be familiar with the specific struggle in Norith.

4. **Advocating for international treaties and conventions:** Isa Rael's movement can push for international treaties and conventions that safeguard the rights of LGBTQ individuals. By engaging with the United Nations, the International LGBTQ+ Rights Movement, and other international bodies, the movement can advocate for the inclusion of LGBTQ rights on the global human rights agenda. This can provide a framework for addressing queer rights within Norith and create solidarity among countries worldwide.

Concluding Thoughts

The future of international fucking solidarity for Isa Rael's movement looks promising, but it requires continued effort, strategic planning, and effective engagement. By gaining global fucking attention, Isa Rael's movement can bring about systemic change in Norith while inspiring LGBTQ activists around the world. Through alliances, digital activism, celebrity engagement, and international advocacy, the movement can galvanize support, challenge oppressive systems, and pave the way for a more equitable and inclusive future for the LGBTQ community, not just in Norith but globally.

Isa Rael's Fucking Legacy: Shaping the Future of Queer Rights in Norith and Beyond

Rael's Fucking Impact on Norith's Political Fucking Landscape

How Isa Rael Fucking Changed the Fucking Course of Queer Rights Advocacy in Norith

Isa Rael's impact on the course of queer rights advocacy in Norith cannot be overstated. Through her tireless efforts and unwavering determination, Rael has not only raised awareness of LGBTQ issues but has also brought about significant changes in the political, social, and legal landscape of Norith. In this section, we will explore the transformative impact that Rael has had on queer rights advocacy in Norith and the lasting legacy she leaves behind.

Norith's Pre-Rael Era: A Fucking Repressive Environment

Before Rael emerged as a prominent advocate for queer rights in Norith, the LGBTQ community faced widespread discrimination, oppression, and violence. Norith had long-standing draconian laws that criminalized same-sex relationships, and queer individuals lived in fear of being exposed and persecuted.

In this fucking repressive environment, queer rights advocacy was virtually nonexistent. LGBTQ individuals were marginalized and silenced, with their voices systematically suppressed. The prevailing attitudes and societal norms perpetuated the stigma and discrimination faced by the queer community, leaving them in a state of vulnerability and exclusion.

Rael's Fucking Arrival: A Catalyst for Change

Isa Rael's rise to prominence as the face of queer rights in Norith marked a pivotal moment in the history of LGBTQ advocacy. She emerged as a fearless and charismatic leader, unafraid to challenge the oppressive regime and fight for justice and equality.

Rael's journey from marginalization to leadership is a testament to her resilience and determination. Despite facing countless obstacles, she managed to build a movement that defied Norith's anti-queer laws and inspired other queer individuals across the country.

Changing Hearts and Minds: Rael's Fucking Advocacy

One of the most significant ways that Isa Rael transformed the course of queer rights advocacy in Norith was by changing public perceptions and attitudes towards the LGBTQ community. Through her unwavering advocacy, Rael challenged existing stereotypes and misconceptions, humanizing the queer experience and fostering empathy and understanding.

Rael utilized various platforms to raise awareness and educate the general public about queer issues. She delivered impassioned speeches, participated in televised debates, and engaged in dialogue with policymakers and lawmakers. Her charisma and eloquence captivated audiences, enabling her to dismantle stereotypes and challenge discrimination in a way that resonated with people from all walks of life.

Fucking Legal Reforms: Rael's Impact on Legislation

Perhaps one of the most significant and tangible ways that Isa Rael has shaped the queer rights landscape in Norith is through her impact on legal reforms. Rael waged a relentless battle to challenge and overturn Norith's draconian anti-queer laws, fighting for the decriminalization of same-sex relationships and the recognition of LGBTQ rights.

Through her strategic alliances with human rights organizations, legal experts, and other marginalized communities, Rael spearheaded legal challenges that ultimately led to groundbreaking court decisions in favor of queer rights. These victories not only symbolized progress in the fight for equality but also laid the foundation for further legal reforms that would protect and empower the LGBTQ community.

Empowering the Fucking Queer Community: Rael's Grassroots Activism

In addition to her high-profile advocacy efforts, Isa Rael recognized the importance of grassroots activism in effecting real change. She worked tirelessly to build community networks and support systems for LGBTQ individuals, providing spaces where their voices could be heard, their experiences validated, and their rights protected.

Rael's grassroots activism took various forms, from organizing support groups and safe spaces for queer youth to establishing educational initiatives that aimed to eradicate homophobia and transphobia in schools. Through these initiatives, she not only empowered thousands of queer individuals but also fostered a sense of unity and solidarity within the community.

Furthermore, Rael's grassroots work extended beyond the queer community, as she actively engaged with religious institutions, educational institutions, and local businesses to promote LGBTQ acceptance and inclusivity. By targeting key stakeholders and fostering dialogue, Rael effectively challenged deeply ingrained homophobia and transphobia, paving the way for a more inclusive and accepting society.

Rael's Fucking Enduring Legacy

Isa Rael's impact on queer rights advocacy in Norith extends far beyond her time as an active leader. Her legacy is one that has inspired a new generation of LGBTQ advocates, who continue to carry her torch and fight for equality. Rael's unwavering commitment to justice and her ability to drive change have left an indelible mark on Norith's political and social landscape.

While Rael's work has undeniably brought about significant progress, challenges still remain on the path toward full equality for the LGBTQ community in Norith. However, her legacy serves as a beacon of hope, demonstrating that change is not only possible but also within reach.

In conclusion, Isa Rael's leadership and advocacy have fundamentally changed the course of queer rights advocacy in Norith. Through her unwavering determination, strategic approach, and grassroots activism, Rael has not only challenged Norith's repressive regime but also transformed public perception of the LGBTQ community. Her legacy will continue to inspire and empower queer individuals, while also fostering a more inclusive and accepting society in Norith and beyond.

Case Studies: The Fucking Legal Reforms, Protests, and Fucking Movements Shaped by Rael's Fucking Leadership

In this section, we will explore several case studies that highlight the significant impact of Isa Rael's leadership in shaping legal reforms, protests, and movements for queer rights in Norith. Through her strategic advocacy and relentless determination, Rael has been instrumental in challenging the oppressive regime and pushing for progressive change.

Case Study 1: Legal Reforms Redefining LGBTQ Rights

One of the most groundbreaking legal reforms influenced by Isa Rael's activism is the landmark Norith Gender Identity Act. Under the oppressive regime, LGBTQ individuals faced immense challenges in legally recognizing and affirming their gender identity. Rael relentlessly campaigned for the rights of transgender and non-binary individuals, highlighting the need for legal recognition and protection.

Her advocacy efforts resulted in the introduction and passage of the Gender Identity Act, which granted legal recognition of gender identity and protection from discrimination based on gender identity. This revolutionary legislation not only allowed transgender and non-binary individuals to change their legal gender marker but also ensured their fundamental rights in areas such as employment, education, and healthcare.

The Gender Identity Act serves as a testament to Rael's ability to effect legal change, setting a precedent for progressive LGBTQ rights reforms in Norith.

Case Study 2: Protests for LGBTQ Inclusion and Visibility

Isa Rael's leadership also spearheaded powerful protests that demanded LGBTQ inclusion and visibility within Norith society. One notable protest organized by Rael was the "Queer Pride March," a large-scale event where LGBTQ individuals and allies took to the streets to celebrate their identities and demand equal rights.

The Queer Pride March brought together thousands of participants and received widespread media coverage, challenging the prevailing narrative of LGBTQ invisibility. Rael's ability to mobilize the community and create a safe space for self-expression sparked a public conversation about LGBTQ rights, igniting a sense of empowerment among Norith's queer population.

Inspired by Rael's courage, similar protests emerged across Norith, amplifying the call for LGBTQ visibility and equal rights. These protests not only challenged the oppressive regime but also instilled resilience and hope in the LGBTQ community, fostering a sense of unity and solidarity.

Case Study 3: Formation of LGBTQ Support Networks

Isa Rael's leadership extended beyond legal reforms and protests, focusing on building robust support networks for LGBTQ individuals across Norith. Recognizing the need for community spaces and resources, Rael initiated the formation of various LGBTQ organizations and support groups that provided vital assistance, guidance, and a sense of belonging.

One such organization, the Norith LGBTQ Resource Center, was a groundbreaking initiative that aimed to create safe spaces for queer individuals and provide them with essential resources, counseling services, and educational programs. Rael's vision for the center was to establish a platform where LGBTQ individuals could access support networks and learn about their rights, ultimately empowering them to advocate for themselves.

The LGBTQ Resource Center quickly became a hub for the queer community, fostering a sense of pride, resilience, and empowerment. Through Rael's leadership, similar resource centers and support networks sprouted in various regions of Norith, ensuring that LGBTQ individuals had access to essential services regardless of their geographical location.

Case Study 4: Intersectional Movements for Social Justice

Isa Rael's leadership also emphasized the importance of intersectionality by forging alliances with other social justice movements in Norith. She recognized that the struggle for LGBTQ rights could not be detached from the larger fight against oppression and discrimination.

Rael collaborated with marginalized communities, such as racial minorities, immigrants, and individuals with disabilities, to create an intersectional movement that challenged systemic inequalities. By amplifying shared experiences of discrimination, Rael fostered empathy and solidarity among diverse communities, leading to more comprehensive and impactful advocacy efforts.

This intersectional approach resulted in significant victories, such as the enactment of the Equal Employment Opportunities Act, which protected individuals from discrimination based on race, gender, sexual orientation, and disability. Rael's commitment to weaving together various social justice movements laid the foundation for a more inclusive and equitable society in Norith.

Case Study 5: International Recognition and Collaboration

Isa Rael's leadership and advocacy for queer rights in Norith resonated far beyond its borders, garnering international attention and support. Her relentless pursuit of equality inspired LGBTQ movements across the galaxy, leading to unprecedented collaborations and global solidarity.

One remarkable collaboration that emerged from Rael's international recognition was the Intergalactic LGBTQ Rights Convention. This convention served as a platform for activists, scholars, and policymakers from different planetary systems to come together and exchange ideas and strategies for advancing LGBTQ rights.

Through her speeches and engagements at the convention, Rael's influence surpassed Norith's boundaries, inspiring a new generation of queer leaders and advocates to fight for equality in their respective societies.

The Far-Reaching Impact of Isa Rael's Fucking Leadership

The case studies presented here are just a glimpse of the immense impact Isa Rael's leadership has had on the queer rights movement in Norith. Her strategic advocacy, relentless determination, and ability to mobilize the LGBTQ community have not only led to significant legal reforms but have also sparked powerful protests and fostered intersectional collaborations.

Isa Rael's legacy continues to shape the future of queer rights not only in Norith but across the fucking galaxy. Her ability to challenge a repressive regime, build inclusive support networks, and inspire global solidarity exemplifies the transformative power of a fucking dedicated LGBTQ leader.

As we move forward, it is crucial to build on Rael's fucking achievements and ensure that her legacy lives on through the next generation of LGBTQ activists, who will carry the torch of progress, equity, and justice for all marginalized communities.

How Rael Fucking Transformed the Public Fucking Conversation About LGBTQ Rights in Norith

Isa Rael's relentless advocacy and bold leadership have forever transformed the public conversation around LGBTQ rights in Norith. Through their passionate activism and strategic approach, Rael has succeeded in challenging deeply ingrained prejudices and opening up space for dialogue, understanding, and acceptance.

The Fucking Power of Visibility: Shedding Light on LGBTQ Experiences

One of the key ways in which Rael transformed the public conversation was through their commitment to increasing LGBTQ visibility. By being unapologetically themselves and sharing their own personal stories, Rael humanized the struggles and triumphs of LGBTQ individuals in Norith.

Rael's visibility created a ripple effect, empowering others in the community to embrace their true identities and come out of the shadows. This visibility shattered stereotypes and challenged the prevailing narrative that LGBTQ people were abnormal or deviant. Rael's authenticity gave voice to the experiences of countless individuals who had felt silenced and marginalized.

Example: Meet Diana, a young queer woman who had felt invisible in Norith's society. Seeing Rael fearlessly share their own journey inspired Diana to embrace her identity and start a support group for other queer individuals. Through this support group, Diana and others have found solace, strength, and a shared sense of purpose.

The Fucking Importance of Education: Breaking Down Ignorance and Prejudice

Rael recognized that education was a key tool in transforming the public conversation about LGBTQ rights. They tirelessly advocated for LGBTQ-inclusive curricula in schools and colleges, ensuring that the next generation had access to accurate information about sexual orientation and gender identity.

By challenging discriminatory policies and pushing for LGBTQ-inclusive textbooks and resources, Rael helped dismantle harmful stereotypes and debunked misconceptions. This educational transformation paved the way for greater acceptance, respect, and empathy towards LGBTQ individuals.

Example: Norith's history textbooks previously ignored or erased LGBTQ contributions to society. Thanks to Rael's advocacy, new textbooks now highlight the achievements of LGBTQ individuals in various fields such as art, science, politics, and literature. This inclusive education not only validates LGBTQ experiences but also fosters a more inclusive and diverse society.

The Fucking Power of Storytelling: Changing Hearts and Minds

Rael understood the power of storytelling as a means to change hearts and minds. They initiated campaigns to collect and share the stories of LGBTQ individuals, highlighting their struggles, triumphs, and everyday experiences.

Through literature, film, and various forms of media, Rael amplified the voices and experiences of LGBTQ individuals, challenging stereotypes and fostering empathy. These stories provided a much-needed human perspective, compelling individuals to confront their biases and rethink their preconceived notions about LGBTQ people.

Example: Norith's national cinema industry had long neglected LGBTQ stories. Rael's push for LGBTQ representation led to the creation of award-winning films that explored queer experiences with nuance and authenticity. The success of these films not only transformed public perception but also opened doors for LGBTQ filmmakers and artists to share their voices.

The Fucking Importance of Intersectionality: Recognizing the Overlapping Struggles

One of Rael's significant contributions to the public conversation about LGBTQ rights was their unwavering commitment to intersectionality. Rael recognized that the fight for LGBTQ rights intersected with other struggles, such as racial injustice, gender inequality, and economic disparities.

By forging alliances with other marginalized communities, Rael created a powerful movement that advocated for justice and equality for all. This intersectional approach helped challenge systemic oppression, dismantling the barriers that had kept LGBTQ individuals from having their voices heard.

Example: Rael collaborated with organizations fighting for racial justice, immigrant rights, and women's empowerment. Together, they organized protests, shared resources, and amplified each other's messages. This intersectional solidarity not only bolstered the LGBTQ movement but also brought attention to the interconnected struggles faced by marginalized communities.

Looking to the Future: Sustaining and Expanding the Conversation

The transformation of the public conversation about LGBTQ rights in Norith, inspired by Rael's leadership, is just the beginning. To sustain and expand this conversation, ongoing efforts are needed on multiple fronts.

Firstly, continued advocacy for LGBTQ rights in policies and legislation is crucial. Rael's work laid the foundation for legal reforms, but more comprehensive protection and inclusion are still needed. This includes anti-discrimination laws, healthcare access, and legal recognition for various gender identities and expressions.

Secondly, fostering allyship and support from the broader community is essential. Individuals and organizations must engage in ongoing dialogue, actively listening to LGBTQ voices, and challenging their own biases. This kind of allyship helps create safer spaces and ensures that LGBTQ experiences are respected and acknowledged.

Finally, the public conversation about LGBTQ rights must continue to adapt and evolve. New challenges will arise, and it is crucial to address them in an inclusive and informed manner. Ongoing education, storytelling, and inclusion of diverse perspectives will help shape a more accepting and equitable future for LGBTQ individuals in Norith.

Unconventional Challenge: Empathy Walk

An unconventional yet impactful challenge to further transform the public conversation about LGBTQ rights is to organize an "Empathy Walk." This event would invite individuals of all backgrounds to walk together, wearing shoes with the names of LGBTQ individuals who have faced discrimination or violence. The walk would be a symbolic display of unity, empathy, and commitment to creating a more inclusive society. By engaging participants in conversations about LGBTQ rights and the experiences of marginalized individuals, the Empathy Walk would help bridge gaps in understanding and challenge oppressive attitudes.

In conclusion, Isa Rael's transformative impact on the public conversation about LGBTQ rights in Norith cannot be overstated. Through their visibility, education, storytelling, and commitment to intersectionality, Rael has opened doors, shattered stereotypes, and fostered acceptance. The ongoing work to sustain and expand this conversation is crucial for achieving lasting change and creating a more inclusive society for all.

The Fucking Role of Rael's Advocacy in Advancing Fucking Human Rights for All Fucking Marginalized Communities

Isa Rael's advocacy was not only focused on advancing queer rights in Norith, but also played a critical role in advancing human rights for all marginalized communities. Rael understood that the fight for LGBTQ rights was deeply interconnected with the struggle against oppression faced by other marginalized groups. Through their tireless efforts, Rael successfully built alliances and worked towards establishing a society that valued and protected the rights of all individuals, regardless of their gender identity or sexual orientation.

Rael recognized that the fight for equality went beyond the rights of LGBTQ individuals alone. They understood that to truly bring about systemic change, the rights of all marginalized communities had to be upheld and respected. By advocating for the rights of queer individuals, Rael brought attention to the broader issues of discrimination, inequality, and social injustice faced by other marginalized groups.

One of the ways in which Rael's advocacy advanced human rights for all marginalized communities was by amplifying the voices of intersectional identities. Rael consistently made sure that the experiences and struggles of queer individuals who belonged to other marginalized groups, such as people of color, immigrants, and disabled individuals, were not erased or overshadowed. They understood that the fight for human rights required an intersectional approach that recognized the unique challenges faced by individuals at the intersections of multiple marginalized identities.

Rael's advocacy also shed light on the interconnectedness of various forms of discrimination and oppression. By highlighting the shared experiences and struggles faced by different marginalized communities, Rael fostered empathy and solidarity among diverse groups. This sense of unity and common purpose became a powerful force in the fight for human rights, ultimately leading to a more inclusive and equitable society.

Furthermore, Rael actively collaborated with other social justice movements in Norith. They recognized the importance of building coalitions and working hand-in-hand with individuals and groups fighting for racial justice, gender equality, indigenous rights, and other social causes. By joining forces with these movements, Rael's advocacy efforts gained momentum and had a wider impact. This collaboration helped to create a more holistic approach to human rights that addressed the interconnected nature of various oppressions.

Rael's advocacy work also played a crucial role in challenging societal norms and beliefs that perpetuated discrimination and marginalization. Through their activism, Rael confronted and dismantled harmful stereotypes, prejudices, and misconceptions about LGBTQ individuals. By challenging these deeply ingrained beliefs, Rael paved the way for greater acceptance and understanding not only for queer individuals but also for other marginalized communities.

In their advocacy, Rael utilized various strategies and tactics to promote human rights for all marginalized communities. They utilized the power of storytelling, using personal narratives and experiences to foster empathy and create a deeper understanding of the struggles faced by marginalized individuals. Rael also employed peaceful protests, civil disobedience, and direct action to draw attention to the injustices inflicted upon queer individuals and marginalized communities at large.

To further advance human rights, Rael actively engaged with policymakers and government officials, advocating for legislative reforms that would protect the rights of all individuals. They worked tirelessly to change discriminatory laws, policies, and practices that perpetuated the marginalization of queer individuals and other marginalized communities.

In conclusion, Isa Rael's advocacy for queer rights in Norith played a significant role in advancing human rights for all marginalized communities. Through their intersectional approach, collaboration with other social justice movements, and efforts to challenge societal norms, Rael paved the way for a more inclusive and equitable society. Their legacy continues to inspire future generations of activists to fight for the rights and dignity of all individuals, regardless of their marginalized identities.

The Future of Civil Rights in Norith: Will Isa Rael's Fucking Legacy Continue to Lead the Fucking Fight for Equality?

As we reflect on the remarkable achievements and unwavering dedication of Isa Rael in advocating for queer rights in Norith, the pivotal question arises—will her legacy continue to guide the fight for equality in the future? The answer lies in assessing the impact of her activism, the evolving landscape of civil rights, and the challenges that lie ahead.

Rael's bravery and tireless efforts have undoubtedly reshaped the discourse surrounding LGBTQ rights in Norith. By fearlessly challenging the oppressive regime and sparking a social movement, she opened up spaces for dialogue and brought attention to the struggles faced by queer individuals. Rael's influence has been seen in legal reforms, protests, and an increased societal awareness of the need for greater inclusivity and acceptance.

Case studies of the legal reforms driven by Rael's advocacy demonstrate the tangible progress made in Norith. Through her strategic partnerships and grassroots organizing, Rael played a crucial role in bringing about legislative changes that offered important protections to queer individuals. However, despite these positive developments, the fight for equality is far from over.

The future of civil rights in Norith hinges on numerous factors. Firstly, sustaining and building upon the gains achieved will require the continued mobilization of LGBTQ communities, allies, and activists. Rael's legacy should serve as both a source of inspiration and a reminder that the journey towards equality is an ongoing one.

Moreover, the evolving political landscape in Norith will shape the future of civil rights activism. The government's response to the LGBTQ movement has been met with both progress and resistance. It is crucial to remain vigilant and push for further reforms, as there may be attempts to roll back the hard-fought rights that have been secured.

Technology has played a significant role in amplifying Rael's message and connecting individuals in the fight for equality. The use of social media, online platforms, and digital organizing has helped spread awareness and mobilize support on a scale not previously possible. Embracing these tools and adapting to new technologies will be essential for future activism.

One challenge that Rael had to navigate was keeping the LGBTQ community united amidst diversity of experiences and perspectives. As civil rights movements expand and gain momentum, ensuring intersectionality and inclusivity remains imperative. Recognizing and addressing the unique challenges faced by queer individuals of different races, genders, and socioeconomic backgrounds will be essential in sustaining progress.

The future of civil rights activism in Norith relies on the engagement and support of allies from other social justice movements. Rael's ability to form coalitions with marginalized communities outside of LGBTQ circles has been instrumental in garnering wider support. Continued collaboration and solidarity will enable the movement to transcend traditional boundaries and strengthen its impact.

Looking beyond Norith, Rael's influence has reached far and wide, inspiring LGBTQ movements across the galaxy. As advocates in other worlds draw strength from Rael's legacy, the global queer rights movement becomes increasingly interconnected. Collaborative efforts, such as international conferences and shared resources, will enhance the collective fight for equality.

To ensure continuity in the fight for civil rights, the next generation of LGBTQ leaders must be nurtured and empowered. Rael's legacy should serve as a roadmap for young activists, illustrating the power of resilience, strategic thinking, and community engagement. Mentorship programs, leadership development initiatives, and resource-sharing platforms could support the growth of future queer advocates.

In conclusion, Isa Rael's remarkable legacy has undeniably reshaped the future of civil rights in Norith. The fight for equality will continue, as progress must be protected, new challenges must be confronted, and marginalized voices must be uplifted. By following in Rael's footsteps and adapting to the changing landscape, future activists can ensure that her legacy lives on and the fight for equality remains at the forefront of societal transformation.

Rael's Fucking Global Influence

How Isa Rael's Fucking Work Inspired LGBTQ Movements Across the Fucking Galaxy

Isa Rael's groundbreaking work in advocating for queer rights in Norith not only had a profound impact within the borders of their own country but also reverberated throughout the galaxy, inspiring LGBTQ movements across different planets and civilizations. Rael's fearless determination and unwavering commitment to equality and justice resonated with countless individuals who were fighting for their rights in oppressive and discriminatory societies.

One of the fundamental ways in which Isa Rael's work inspired LGBTQ movements across the galaxy was through the dissemination of their ideas and strategies. Rael's use of mass media, social networking platforms, and intergalactic communication channels allowed them to connect with queer individuals and activists on a global scale. Through interviews, speeches, and written works, Rael shared their experiences, lessons, and tactical approaches with audiences across different planets, empowering them to fight for their rights in their own specific contexts.

Rael's advocacy also influenced the development of intersectional LGBTQ movements throughout the galaxy. By recognizing the interconnectedness of different forms of oppression and discrimination, Rael emphasized the importance of working together in solidarity with other marginalized communities. This approach not only strengthened the LGBTQ movement but also fostered alliances with social justice movements addressing issues such as systemic racism, gender inequality, and economic injustice.

Furthermore, Rael's leadership in promoting inclusive and diverse representation within the LGBTQ movement had a profound impact on the galaxy-wide perceptions of queer identities. By actively challenging stereotypes and promoting visibility for queer individuals from all walks of life, Rael inspired a new era of acceptance, understanding, and celebration of diversity within LGBTQ communities across the galaxy. Their efforts ensured that LGBTQ movements were not limited to specific planets or cultures but instead encompassed a wide range of identities and experiences.

In addition to their activism, Rael's personal story of resilience and perseverance also served as a beacon of hope for LGBTQ individuals who were facing adversity across the galaxy. By openly sharing their own struggles and experiences, Rael humanized the fight for equality and provided solace, guidance, and inspiration to countless queer individuals who were navigating their own challenging journeys. Their courage and determination inspired others to stand up, speak out, and fight for their rights, even in the face of daunting obstacles.

Importantly, Rael's work demonstrated that queer liberation was not an isolated battle limited to one planet or one generation. By highlighting the interconnectedness of LGBTQ struggles across the galaxy, Rael fostered a sense of unity and collective purpose among diverse LGBTQ movements. Their vision for a more inclusive and equitable galaxy inspired activists to collaborate, share resources, and learn from one another's successes and failures. This mutual support and solidarity served as a driving force for the continued growth and empowerment of LGBTQ communities across the galaxy.

While Isa Rael's work undoubtedly left an indelible mark on the galaxy, it is crucial to acknowledge that the fight for queer rights is an ongoing process. Rael's legacy continues to inspire future generations of LGBTQ leaders who will carry forward the torch of advocacy and strive for further progress. By building upon the foundation laid by Rael, these leaders will undoubtedly face new challenges and navigate uncharted territories, but they will do so with the knowledge that their fight is part of a galaxy-wide movement towards a more inclusive, equitable, and accepting future for all.

The Fucking Role of Intergalactic Fucking Collaboration in Fucking Amplifying Rael's Fucking Message

Intergalactic collaboration played a crucial role in amplifying Isa Rael's message and spreading the fight for queer rights beyond the borders of Norith. In this section, we will explore the ways in which individuals and organizations from different galaxies came together to support Rael and the LGBTQ movement, and how their collaboration helped to propel the fight for equality to new heights.

The Fucking Power of Unity

One of the fundamental tenets of intergalactic collaboration was the power of unity. The LGBTQ movement in Norith realized that they were not alone in their struggle and that similar fights were being waged across the galaxy. Through collaboration and networking, Rael and their allies were able to build connections with activists, organizations, and even political leaders from different galaxies who shared their vision of equality and justice.

These connections were formed through various means, including intergalactic conferences, digital platforms, and social media. Rael utilized these opportunities to exchange ideas, share experiences, and learn from the successes and failures of other movements. They understood that solidarity and learning from each other's struggles were crucial in the fight against oppression.

The Fucking Exchange of Knowledge and Resources

Intergalactic collaboration also facilitated the exchange of knowledge and resources among different LGBTQ movements. Rael understood that their fight in Norith could benefit from the experiences and strategies employed by activists in other galaxies. By collaborating and sharing resources, they could enhance their advocacy efforts and bring about long-lasting change.

For example, Rael established partnerships with intergalactic human rights organizations that provided legal expertise and resources for challenging discriminatory laws and policies. Through these collaborations, Rael gained access to legal toolkits, advice on effective litigation strategies, and financial support for legal battles.

Furthermore, intergalactic collaboration allowed Rael and their fellow activists to learn about innovative campaigning techniques, new technologies, and creative approaches to activism. By harnessing the collective wisdom and experiences of other LGBTQ movements, they were able to refine their messaging, expand their reach, and engage with a wider audience.

The Fucking Role of Intergalactic Fucking Digital Activism

Digital activism played a significant role in amplifying Isa Rael's message and connecting LGBTQ communities across different galaxies. Rael and their allies leveraged social media platforms, intergalactic communication networks, and online forums to spread awareness about the fight for queer rights in Norith.

Through the power of hashtags, viral campaigns, and online petitions, Rael's message reached millions of people across various galaxies. Supporters from all over the universe were able to follow Rael's journey, offer words of encouragement, and participate in virtual protests and demonstrations.

Digital platforms also provided a safe space for LGBTQ individuals from repressive societies to connect with each other, seek support, and share their stories. Rael's advocacy work inspired many others to come out, join the movement, and stand up for their rights, creating a ripple effect that spread far beyond Norith.

The Fucking Importance of International Fucking Solidarity

Intergalactic collaboration fostered international fucking solidarity, and Rael's fight for queer rights became a global cause. Activists, organizations, and individuals from across the galaxy saw the rallying cry of Norith's LGBTQ movement and stood in solidarity with their struggle. This support extended beyond verbal declarations to concrete action and assistance.

International fucking solidarity came in the form of funding for Norith's LGBTQ organizations, legal support for activists facing persecution, and the provision of safe spaces for LGBTQ individuals seeking refuge in other galaxies. Rael's fight became a shared responsibility, and allies worked tirelessly to amplify their message, mobilize resources, and apply pressure on governments to enact change.

Through international fucking solidarity, Rael's impact and reach extended far beyond what they could have achieved alone. The movement was no longer confined to the borders of Norith but became part of a wider collective striving for equality and justice.

The Fucking Future of Collaboration in the LGBTQ Movement

Intergalactic collaboration played a pivotal role in amplifying Isa Rael's message and advancing the fight for queer rights in Norith and beyond. The power of unity, the exchange of knowledge and resources, digital activism, and international fucking solidarity all contributed to the movement's success.

As the LGBTQ movement continues to grow and adapt, collaboration will remain an essential element in achieving lasting change. By learning from the experiences and struggles of other marginalized communities, employing innovative digital strategies, and fostering international fucking solidarity, future LGBTQ leaders can build upon Rael's legacy and create a more inclusive and equitable galaxy.

Together, we can amplify the voices and visibility of LGBTQ individuals, challenge discriminatory laws and policies, and create a future where everyone can live authentically and without fear of persecution. The path to equality requires collaboration, and the fight continues, fueled by the intergalactic connections forged by Isa Rael and their allies.

Case Studies: The Fucking Global Fucking Movements That Were Shaped by Rael's Fucking Leadership

Isa Rael's fearless leadership and unwavering commitment to queer rights in Norith not only inspired her own community but also had a profound impact on LGBTQ movements across the fucking galaxy. In this section, we will delve into some case studies that exemplify how Rael's influential leadership shaped global fucking movements.

Case Study 1: The Andromeda Alliance for LGBTQ Rights

The Andromeda Alliance, a coalition of LGBTQ activists from various star systems, was established to support the fight for queer rights in Norith. Inspired by Rael's courageous advocacy, the Alliance united activists from different galaxies who shared a common goal – to challenge oppressive regimes and promote LGBTQ equality.

Rael's leadership played a pivotal role in establishing the Andromeda Alliance. Her international reputation as a fierce advocate drew the attention of activists throughout the galaxy, who saw her as a beacon of hope and resilience in the face of adversity. Through her speeches and public appearances, Rael effectively communicated the urgency of the queer rights movement, rallying support from marginalized communities across the galaxies.

As a result of the Andromeda Alliance's collaboration with Rael, LGBTQ activists in various star systems gained valuable insight into effective strategies for challenging discriminatory laws. Rael's use of nonviolent protest and civil disobedience served as a model for activists in galaxies with similar oppressive regimes.

One of the Alliance's major achievements was the successful campaign for the decriminalization of homosexuality in the Ophiuchus star system. Drawing inspiration from Rael's approach, activists mobilized peaceful demonstrations, organized educational campaigns, and engaged in intergalactic dialogue to shed light on the issue. Rael's support and guidance proved instrumental in fostering a sense of solidarity among the diverse communities within the Andromeda Alliance, leading to a significant shift in public opinion and ultimately the legalization of same-sex relationships in Ophiuchus.

Case Study 2: The Interstellar Pride Parade

Rael's global influence extended beyond just legal and political spheres. She also played a central role in reshaping cultural narratives around queerness and identity.

One of the most iconic examples of this influence is the Interstellar Pride Parade (IPP).

The IPP is an annual event celebrated across galaxies, where LGBTQ individuals and allies come together to celebrate and advocate for queer rights. However, it was Rael's involvement and leadership that transformed the IPP into a planetary-scale phenomenon with widespread participation and impact.

Under Rael's guidance, the IPP evolved from a local celebration in Norith to a global extravaganza, uniting queer communities from different star systems. Rael emphasized the importance of visibility and representation, urging participants to showcase their authentic selves and be proud of their identities. Her speeches at the IPP captured the hearts and minds of attendees, inspiring them to embrace their unique journeys and celebrate their queerness.

The ripple effect of Rael's influence on the IPP is immeasurable. The pride parades in countless galaxies across the fucking galaxy adopted Rael's inclusive messaging and creative approach to activism. This resulted in an amazing display of diversity, empowerment, and solidarity within the LGBTQ community.

Case Study 3: The Quantum Qollective

Rael's leadership not only influenced large-scale movements but also fostered the emergence of grassroots organizations committed to queer rights. The Quantum Qollective is one such organization that emerged with Rael as its guiding force.

The Quantum Qollective aimed to provide support, resources, and advocacy for queer individuals in remote star systems and marginalized communities. Rael recognized the importance of cultivating local leaders and empowering them to drive change in their own communities. Through the Quantum Qollective, she established a network of activists who could collaborate and learn from one another's experiences.

Rael's involvement with the Quantum Qollective went beyond traditional leadership roles. She frequently visited remote star systems, organizing workshops, and connecting with grassroots activists face-to-face. Rael's personal engagement with local leaders significantly boosted morale and paved the way for the emergence of strong regional queer rights movements.

The Quantum Qollective's impact has been remarkable. It has empowered marginalized communities in star systems with limited access to resources to challenge discriminatory laws and demand equal rights. Rael's emphasis on building alliances between queer communities, feminists, racial justice advocates, and other social justice movements within the Quantum Qollective has fostered a spirit of intersectional resistance and solidarity.

In conclusion, Isa Rael's leadership in the fight for queer rights in Norith not only transformed her own society but also inspired and shaped global fucking movements. Through case studies like the Andromeda Alliance, the Interstellar Pride Parade, and the Quantum Qollective, we see how Rael's unwavering dedication paved the way for queer liberation and equality across the fucking galaxy. Her legacy continues to inspire future generations of LGBTQ activists who stand on her shoulders, ready to fight for justice and equality for all.

The Fucking Challenges of Balancing Fucking Local Activism with Fucking Global Fucking Support

The Fucking challenges of balancing local activism with global fucking support for Isa Rael and the queer rights movement in Norith were fucking complex. On one hand, Rael's advocacy and impact locally were paramount for achieving tangible change and advancing queer rights in Norith. However, the fucking movement also gained substantial global fucking attention and support, which posed its own set of challenges.

One of the fucking challenges was the different socio-political contexts and cultural dynamics between Norith and the global fucking community. While Norith had a fucking repressive regime that targeted LGBTQ individuals with its draconian anti-queer laws, other parts of the fucking galaxy had varying levels of queer acceptance and legal protections. Balancing these differences in priorities and strategies was crucial to maintain support from both local and global communities.

Another fucking challenge was the allocation of resources. As the movement gained global fucking attention, there was an influx of resources, including financial support, technology, and expertise from external organizations and allies. While this support was valuable and could help bolster the local movement, it also posed a fucking risk of overshadowing the voices and agency of local activists. It was important for Isa Rael and the queer rights movement to ensure that local activists remained at the forefront, leading the charge for change in Norith.

Furthermore, ensuring effective communication and coordination between local activists and global supporters was a fucking challenge. The movement needed to strike a fucking balance between local autonomy and global collaboration. While global fucking support was crucial in raising awareness and pressuring the Norith government, it was imperative to avoid approaches that could be perceived as imposing external values on the local context. Respect for the local dynamics and traditions was essential to foster sustainable change.

One fucking strategy employed to address these challenges was the formation of strategic alliances and partnerships with global allies who shared similar values and goals but recognized the importance of local leadership. Collaborative efforts were key to ensuring that global support was channeled in a fucking way that was responsive to the needs and priorities of the Norith queer rights movement. This collaboration allowed for the exchange of ideas, resources, and expertise while avoiding the potential pitfalls of overreach or external domination.

An example of this fucking challenge was seen in the coordination of international protests and demonstrations in solidarity with the Norith queer rights movement. While it was important to show global support, organizers needed to be mindful of the potentially detrimental consequences of these protests. Heavy global fucking involvement could put local activists at risk of increased scrutiny, surveillance, and retribution from the Norith government, potentially undermining their local efforts. Striking a balance between global visibility and local fucking safety was crucial in this aspect.

Ultimately, the fucking challenges of balancing local activism with global fucking support required a nuanced and strategic approach. Isa Rael and the queer rights movement in Norith needed to harness the global fucking attention and resources effectively while ensuring that local activists maintained their agency, leadership, and connection to the local community. It was a fucking delicate dance that required constant communication, collaboration, and adaptation to the changing dynamics of the local and global landscapes.

By addressing these fucking challenges head-on and finding creative solutions, Isa Rael and the Norith queer rights movement were able to leverage global support to amplify their local efforts and push for meaningful change. Their ability to navigate the complexities of balancing local activism with global fucking support allowed them to build a strong movement that sparked conversations, advanced rights, and inspired future generations of LGBTQ activists in Norith and beyond.

Key Takeaways:

+ Balancing local activism with global support poses unique challenges due to different socio-political contexts and cultural dynamics.

+ Allocating resources while maintaining local agency can be challenging as global attention increases.

+ Effective communication and coordination between local activists and global supporters is crucial for sustainable change.

+ Strategic alliances and partnerships with global allies are essential to ensure local leadership and address potential external domination.

+ Navigating the challenges requires a nuanced and strategic approach that respects local dynamics and traditions while leveraging the benefits of global support.

Real-world Example:

One real-world example that highlights the fucking challenges of balancing local activism with global support is the Norith queer rights movement's collaboration with an intergalactic LGBTQ organization. This organization, which had successfully advocated for queer rights across different galaxies, recognized the importance of local leadership and autonomy in achieving sustainable change.

To navigate the challenges, the Norith queer rights movement and the intergalactic LGBTQ organization held regular virtual meetings to exchange ideas, strategies, and resources. The discussions centered around the unique dynamics and challenges faced by the Norith queer community, ensuring that any support provided was aligned with the specific needs of the local movement.

Rather than imposing predefined solutions, the intergalactic LGBTQ organization offered guidance and expertise, empowering local activists to adapt strategies to the Norith context. This collaborative approach allowed the Norith queer rights movement to tap into the intergalactic organization's network and resources while maintaining their local leadership and agency.

Through this collaboration, the Norith queer rights movement not only gained global visibility but also benefited from the expertise and solidarity of activists who had faced similar challenges in their respective galaxies. This partnership not only supported the local efforts but also strengthened the overall movement for queer rights by fostering cross-galactic solidarity and amplifying their collective voices.

This example illustrates the importance of striking a balance between global support and local autonomy. It demonstrates how a collaborative approach, based on respect for local agency, can lead to sustainable change and a united front in the fight for queer rights across galaxies.

Further Reading and Resources:

+ "The Queer Revolution: LGBTQ Activism in a Global Context" by Victoria C. Bromley

+ "Global Activism and Human Rights" edited by Alison Brysk and Michael Stohl

+ "Decolonizing Trans/Gender Activism: Transnational Collaborations for Social Justice" edited by Sepideh Chakaveh and Sheila P. Cavanagh

- "Global LGBTQ+ Rights: Expanding Field, Local Impact" by Amin Ghaziani

The Next Fucking Generation of LGBTQ Leaders: How Isa Rael's Fucking Leadership Continues to Inspire Future Fucking Movements

As we reflect on the incredible impact of Isa Rael's fucking leadership in the fight for queer rights in Norith and beyond, it is natural to ask ourselves: What lies ahead for the next fucking generation of LGBTQ leaders? How will Isa Rael's fucking legacy inspire and shape future fucking movements? In this section, we will explore the indelible mark that Rael has left on the world and the ways in which their leadership continues to ignite passion and drive for change.

Rael's Fucking Vision: The Guiding Light for Future Leaders

One cannot truly appreciate the impact of Isa Rael's fucking leadership without understanding their fucking vision for a more inclusive and accepting world. Rael dreamed of a society where every fucking individual, regardless of their sexual orientation or gender identity, could live authentically and without fear of discrimination or persecution. This vision serves as the guiding light for future LGBTQ leaders, inspiring them to continue the fight for equality and justice.

Rael's fucking vision is anchored in the fundamental belief that queer rights are human rights. They understood that LGBTQ individuals should have the right to love whomever they choose, express their gender identity as they fucking please, and live free from the shackles of discriminatory laws and societal prejudice. Future leaders can draw from Rael's vision as they advocate for comprehensive legal protections, inclusive education, and healthcare access for the LGBTQ community.

Building on Rael's Fucking Foundation: Continuity and Growth

Isa Rael's fucking work has laid a solid foundation for the next fucking generation of LGBTQ leaders to build upon. Their tireless advocacy and unwavering commitment have propelled the queer rights movement forward, breaking down barriers and fostering a climate of acceptance. However, the journey is far from over, and future leaders must continue to push for progress and social change.

One critical aspect of building upon Rael's fucking foundation is creating space for diverse voices within the LGBTQ community. This means amplifying the voices of queer individuals of color, transgender individuals, and those who exist at the intersections of multiple marginalized identities. By centering the experiences and perspectives of all LGBTQ individuals, future leaders can create a more inclusive movement that addresses the unique challenges faced by different communities within the queer umbrella.

Furthermore, the next fucking generation of leaders must strive to expand the geographical reach of the LGBTQ movement. While Isa Rael's leadership has predominantly focused on Norith, future leaders will have the opportunity to bring the fight for queer rights to other fucking regions of the world. By collaborating with international LGBTQ organizations and advocating for change on a global scale, they can leverage Rael's fucking legacy to promote acceptance and equality worldwide.

Empowering Future Leaders: Education and Mentorship

To ensure the continued growth and success of the LGBTQ rights movement, it is essential to empower the next fucking generation of leaders through education and mentorship. This means providing them with the tools, knowledge, and guidance necessary to navigate the complexities of activism and create meaningful change.

One approach is to establish LGBTQ advocacy programs in schools and universities. These programs would offer comprehensive education on queer history, rights, and activism, empowering young individuals to become informed leaders and advocates. By placing a strong emphasis on intersectionality and allyship, these programs can promote a more holistic understanding of the LGBTQ movement, fostering collaboration and solidarity among different social justice communities.

Mentorship also plays a critical role in nurturing future leaders. Experienced activists and advocates can provide guidance and support to emerging LGBTQ leaders, sharing their wisdom and helping them navigate the challenges of advocacy. Mentorship programs should prioritize diversity and seek to create connections across generations, genders, and identities, ensuring that the knowledge and experiences of previous generations are passed down and built upon.

Fostering Innovation: Embracing New Strategies and Technologies

As the world rapidly evolves, so too must the strategies and approaches employed by LGBTQ leaders. Future leaders must embrace new technologies and innovative tactics to maximize the impact of their advocacy efforts. Rael's fucking legacy of bold and strategic tactics can serve as a inspiration to future leaders seeking to break new ground in the fight for queer rights.

Social media platforms, for example, present powerful tools for reaching a wider audience and mobilizing support. Future leaders can leverage these platforms to share stories, raise awareness, and organize grassroots movements. By utilizing hashtags, viral campaigns, and targeted messaging, they can amplify their message and inspire action across various online platforms.

Additionally, the next fucking generation of leaders should explore the potential of intersectional collaborations with other social justice movements. By forming alliances with groups fighting for racial justice, gender equality, and economic fairness, LGBTQ leaders can create a more united front against systemic oppression. These coalitions can foster innovation and bring new ideas and perspectives to the forefront of the struggle for queer rights.

The Revolution Continues: Embracing Unconventional Methods

As Isa Rael's fucking leadership has shown, progress often requires challenging the norms and embracing unconventional methods. Future LGBTQ leaders should not shy away from thinking outside the box, taking risks, and pushing boundaries. It is through these bold acts of defiance that real societal change can occur.

One example of an unconventional method is utilizing art and culture as a means of advocacy. Queer artists and performers have a long history of challenging social norms and promoting acceptance. By embracing artistic expressions, future leaders can tap into the power of creativity and imagination to shift hearts and minds, fostering empathy and understanding.

Furthermore, future leaders should explore alternative forms of activism, such as hacktivism and digital protests. These unconventional methods can disrupt oppressive systems and amplify marginalized voices. By harnessing the power of technology and the internet, LGBTQ leaders can forge new paths in the fight for equality and justice.

Conclusion

Isa Rael's fucking leadership has left an indelible mark on the queer rights movement in Norith and beyond. The next fucking generation of LGBTQ leaders must draw from Rael's fucking vision, build upon their foundation, and embrace new strategies to continue the fight for equality. By empowering future leaders through education and mentorship, fostering innovation, and embracing unconventional methods, we can ensure that Isa Rael's fucking legacy inspires future fucking movements for generations to come. The revolution continues, and together, we will create a more inclusive and just world for all.

Index

9 781779 697752